TASMANIAN
DEVIL

BASS STRAIT
TASMANIA
KING IS
FLINDERS IS
BADGER IS
CAPE BARREN IS
CLARKE IS
HUNTER IS
THREE HUMMOCK IS
ROBBINS IS
Stanley
Marrawah
Redpa
HWY
BASS
Trowutta
Arthur River
Arthur R
Temma
Wynyard
Burnie
NARAWNTAPU NAT. PARK
HIGHWAY
Devonport
Waratah
MURCHISON
Trowunna WILDLIFE PARK
Mole Creek
Cradle
Greens Beach
George Town
Tamar R
TASMAN
Launceston
Perth
MIDLAND
BEN LOMOND NAT. PARK
WATERHOUSE CONSERVATION AREA
Bridport
Waterhouse
Cape Portland
Musselroe Bay
Mt William
Pyengana
HWY

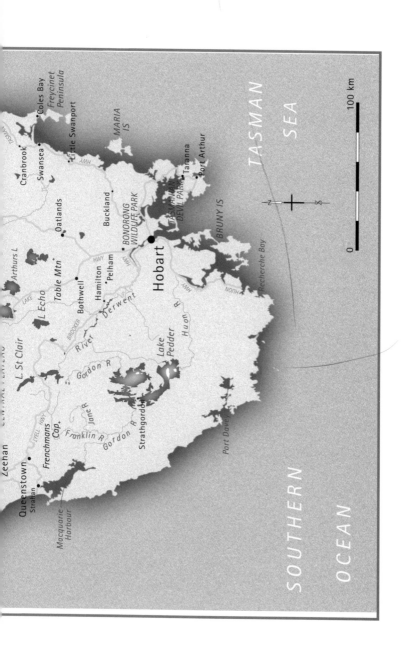

First published in Australia in 2005

Allen & Unwin
83 Alexander Street
Crows Nest NSW 2065
Australia
Phone: (61 2) 8425 0100
Fax: (61 2) 9906 2218
Email: info@allenandunwin.com
Web: www.allenandunwin.com

National Library of Australia
Cataloguing-in-Publication entry:

Owen, David, 1956– .
    Tasmanian devil : a unique and threatened animal.

    Includes index.
    ISBN 1 74114 368 3.

    1. Tasmanian devil. 2. Endangered species – Tasmania.
    I. Pemberton, David. II. Title.

599.27

Typeset in 11/14.5pt Garamond 3 by Midland Typesetters, Maryborough, Victoria
Printed by Ligare Book Printer, Sydney

10 9 8 7 6 5 4 3 2

TASMANIAN DEVIL

A UNIQUE AND THREATENED ANIMAL

DAVID OWEN AND DAVID PEMBERTON

ALLEN&UNWIN

For Leisha, Hilton and Larry
D.O.

For Rosemary, my partner in love, life and field biology
D.P.

CONTENTS

ACKNOWLEDGMENTS

Many organisations and individuals have been of assistance to us in our work on this book, through permission to reproduce words or images and through personal communications.

In particular, and as will be seen throughout the book, Nick Mooney, Tasmanian government wildlife biologist and a long-time advocate of protecting the island's fauna and unique environment, holds a special place in the story of the Tasmanian devil.

Likewise, zoologist and academic Dr Eric Guiler, devoted himself for over fifty years to championing the cause of Tasmania's wildlife, and his pioneering research into the Tasmanian devil remains of seminal importance.

Dr Menna Jones and Androo Kelly are two other Tasmanians who, in contrasting ways, continue to work closely with the Tasmanian devil and whose insights into its behaviour and ecology have significantly increased our understanding of this rare marsupial carnivore.

The tragedy of Devil Facial Tumour Disease (DFTD) threatens the species, challenging its survival. A great variety of individuals, whether working in laboratories or in the field, have spent countless hours in efforts to combat this threat. As joint authors of the Tasmanian devil story we have been acutely conscious of its perilous position, and this has made us all the more aware of the importance of those striving to help it. Their efforts cannot be underestimated, nor should they be undervalued. Thanks in particular in the preparation of this book are extended to Clare Hawkins, Billie Lazenby and Jason Wiersma.

Special thanks to Kathryn Medlock for her advice on the manuscript, to Christo Baars for permission to use his stunning devil images, and to Simon Bevilacqua for his enduring persistence in tracking the devil story.

We also wish to acknowledge and thank: Ian Bowring, Karen Gee, Catherine Taylor, Emma Cotter, Allen & Unwin; Bill Bleathman, Brian Looker, Belinda Bauer, Debbie Robertson, Tasmanian Museum and Art Gallery; Garry Bailey, Editor, *The Mercury*; Steven M. Fogelson, Senior Attorney, Warner Bros. Consumer Products Inc.; Patrick Medway, National President, Wildlife Preservation Society of Australia; Grant Williams, Rokeby Primary School; Toren Virgis, Bonorong Wildlife Park; Elaine Kirchner, Fort Wayne Children's Zoo; Angela Anderson, Tasmanian Devil Park; Tony Marshall, Margaret Harman, State Library of Tasmania; Garth Wigston, Wigston's Lures; Judy K. Long, The Wolverine Foundation; Cheryl Vogt, Wilderness Safaris; Daniel J. Cox, Natural Exposures Inc.; Rob Giason, Tourism Tasmania; Ingrid Albion; Mike Archer; Bill Brown; Max Cameron; Donna Coleman; Rodney Croome; George Davis; Tim Dub; Rosemary Gales; Brian George; Lionel Grey; Lynda Guy; Lois Hall; Maureen Johnstone; Geoff King; Brendan McCrossen; Kate Mooney; Mike Myers; Jenny Nurse; Richard Perry; David Randall; Genene Randell; Steve Randell; Debbie

Sadler; Alan Scott; Garry Sutton; John Teasdale; Russell Wheeldon; John R. Wilson; Stephen Wroe; Dave Watts; Janet Weaving.

DO and DP

INTRODUCTION

These days, I live on a small private nature reserve in the Tasmanian highlands, where a whole family of wicked-looking though loveable black beasts regularly invite themselves to feast at my tent, sometimes around midday with the sun shining through their red ears, often in the dead of night, dressed as they are for darkness and cocktails . . . Some say Tassie devils are innately convicts, thieves and criminals, but I prefer to think they are nature's creatures of fortune, as boisterous and inquisitive as children, who enjoy each other's company, laugh at their own jokes, and share what they find. For what else would they have done with those five missing shoes, champagne bottle, and two billiard balls?

JOHN R. WILSON, QUOIBA

Tasmanian Devil: A unique and threatened animal is the story of a wild animal, the world's largest living marsupial carnivore, about which we have limited understanding. Now there is a tragic possibility that it may become extinct in the wild, or extinct altogether, before we know much more. Sadder still, human activity may be behind the mysterious disease that has decimated the species in the only place in the world where it still exists, the island of Tasmania. Just a few short years ago it was unthinkable that the robust and protected Tasmanian devil might be about to follow in the doom-laden footsteps of its larger relative, the thylacine—a predator that was in large measure rendered extinct by government-sanctioned persecution. This, the first comprehensive book on the Tasmanian devil, is the vibrant, sometimes horrifying, but remarkable story of an iconic marsupial mammal and the great variety of people who have loved, loathed and misunderstood it for centuries.

Marrawah is a coastal township in the far northwest of Tasmania. Late in the twentieth century a fifth-generation Marrawah farmer, Geoff King, elected to cease using his 830-acre property for cattle farming. Instead, he turned it into a wildlife sanctuary, specifically to protect the Tasmanian devil. Much of 'King's Run' fronts wild, rocky coastline. A slow, bumpy ride through scrub takes visitors to his 'devil restaurant': a tiny old white wooden shack close to the surf and protected by extraordinary slabs of multi-hued granite. The area is of strong Aboriginal significance and has an ethereal, otherworld quality about it.

Geoff King and his visitors chat, eat and drink in the crude but comfortable little one-room shack. Outside, near the window, a spotlit wallaby carcass is staked to the ground. A microphone will alert the guests to arriving devils—and they generally turn up, long after dark, hence the pleasure of socialising while waiting, briefly remote from civilisation. As often as not, it will be raining and blowing. The magnified crunching of the devils, and their black-white, sharp but transient interactions with one another, half in and half out of manmade light as they go about their complex feeding business, is vivid and magical, like the sacred area itself, with wind and pounding surf as constant background.

Great tracts of Tasmania are unpopulated, with many areas inaccessible. The King experience provides a surprisingly close natural encounter with a rare animal that even today is wrongly assumed to be aggressive and antisocial and—until its recent devastation—a rural pest. To what extent can we come to know the true devil? As a voyage of devil discovery, this book attempts to answer the question. References are included to most devil literature, good and bad. The devil discoveries, opinions and experiences of experts and casual observers are contained in these pages.

Prior to 1803, the year in which Europeans settled in the island then known as Van Diemen's Land, the devil was known only to the island's 4000 or so indigenous people. There is no documented record of the interactions between those people and the hunter– scavenger carnivore, which was as widespread across the island as were the nine tribes, although archaeological records show that humans and devils used the same cave systems as shelters. All that we have are a few phonetic recordings by early Europeans of the names they heard used for the devil by various tribes, including *tar-de-bar* (or tarrabah), *pile-lin-ner* (or poirinnah) and *par-loo-mer-rer*.

In the two centuries since then, just a small number of individuals can be described as being true devil experts, through their professional dedication to the animal over a substantial period, including much time in the field. They are academic and zoologist Eric Guiler, wildlife officer Nick Mooney, zoologist and curator David Pemberton, marsupial specialist Menna Jones and Trowunna Wildlife Park owner Androo Kelly.

A larger, but still select group of people, have had intimacy with the devil forced upon them tragically, through the spread of devil facial tumour disease, DFTD, the disease that has been killing the animal in increasing numbers since at least the mid-1990s. From the laboratory to the field, dozens of scientists, zoologists, veterinarians, specialist volunteers and bureaucrats are combined in an effort to find the cause of and a cure for DFTD, a virulent facial cancer which causes great suffering and which kills within five months of its manifestation.

A third category knows intimately a different kind of devil, namely, those people who engage with the animal through the daily course of their professions. Tasmanian farmers have the longest unbroken relationship with the devil since European settlement, stretching back 200 years, and even today their opinions of it range from respect to indifference to antagonism. Wildlife park operators are devil experts of another stripe, because they own and nurture the animals in their care, whether captive-born or brought in as surviving dependents of a roadkill mother. Mary Roberts, who operated a zoo in Hobart in the early twentieth century, appreciated the devil like no one before her, and she holds an important place in the devil's story as the first person to study and write about them in detail.

There are also academic experts: the number of postgraduate research students at the University of Tasmania and elsewhere has grown sharply since the first doctoral thesis on the animal was conferred in 1991.

And then there are those for whom the devil has been—or one day will be—a brief encounter. Only rarely are they seen by day in the wild, hence the attraction of the state's increasing number of wildlife parks, which inevitably have devils as the star attraction. To observe three or four in a wildlife park enclosure is a highly controlled experience, but even so, whether dozing, sunbaking, splashing in water, chasing one another or competitively bolting food at mealtime, they are the real thing, almost within touching distance.

The devil's restricted habitat, the absence of devils in overseas zoos, and Tasmania's geographical remoteness—the island is closer to the Antarctic than it is to Darwin—mean that very few people have seen a live Tasmanian devil, far fewer still in the wild. (And until the onset of DFTD, Tasmanians themselves generally thought little about or of the animal.) By contrast Warner Bros.' cartoon character Taz the Tasmanian Devil, a whirling, brown, slobbering creature, has vast international recognition. This compelling paradox is an integral part of the story. Unfortunately, for many Australians the devil is no more than a two-dimensional symbol of the island's identity—even though it has been extinct on the mainland for less than 500 years. Like the thylacine's, the devil's abstracted image can become overwhelming, reducing and belittling the importance of the animal itself.

This book gets as close as it is possible to get to the Tasmanian devil. It is written with great respect for the animal which, until recently, seemed to represent a tremendous evolutionary success story in an ancient continent with a harsh environment. Yet the disease so gravely afflicting the species indicates that, far from being a robust carnivore with no predator species to fear, it is highly vulnerable, and a stark reminder of how limited is our understanding of the unpredictable natural world.

Most difficult of all to describe is the evolutionary 'fitness' of the Tasmanian devil, its 'success' as a species. On the one hand it has flourished for tens of thousands of years throughout its island home. Yet that is the result of a negative evolutionary outcome, its range shrinking from all parts of the continent until a remnant population died out in Victoria. Furthermore, island carnivores are among the most vulnerable of isolated species.

But the disease has shown us a glimpse of remarkable devil behaviour. Evidence has emerged that, in response to the decimation of their numbers, devils have tended to become semelparous: males are breeding when much younger—so taking the place of older males dying while still in their mating prime—but as a result are themselves dying after their first and only litter is weaned. Previously seen only in mammals in the related antechinuses and possibly quolls, it appears to be a natural response to prevent the reproductive cycle from being fatally broken. In human terms we might salute these as acts of supreme self-sacrifice for the greater good. And there is another aspect of the devil's behaviour operating in its favour. Time after time, field biologists dealing with sick and dying devils report a tenacious individual will to survive, including emaciated, cancer-ridden mothers weaning to the point of death. Tasmanian devils don't give up.

David Owen
David Pemberton
2005

1 BEELZEBUB'S PUP: A REAPPRAISAL OF THE TASMANIAN DEVIL

Over the years it got to be a war between Dawn and the devils as the stones, wires and other defences around the house foundations got bigger and bigger. Most years, however, the devils won. The growling would be heard and on inspection next morning they had dug their way through the stones and rocks to get back to their nest. Some nights the noise from the devils was amazing. Dawn had a big stick that she would bang on the lounge room floor to quieten them down . . .

DEBBIE SADLER, ORIELTON

Good stories, no matter how unalike, share a tried and tested formula: intriguing setting; protagonist (good guy) and antagonist (bad guy); plot strength through mystery, drama and action; climax and resolution. In 1863 Morton Allport, a respected Hobart solicitor and naturalist, wrote a letter to his son Curzon describing a trip he had undertaken with a companion into Tasmania's alpine wilderness. An incidental paragraph of that letter exactly covers this formula, in small, slightly slanted handwriting:

> Before leaving Boviak Beach [setting], Packer [good guy] was considerably scared [drama] at meeting [action] what he called a Beelzebub's pup [mystery], in other words, a Tasmanian devil [bad guy], near to the camp but it made off [resolution] before the gun was ready [climax, suspended].[1]

The story of the Tasmanian devil is a remarkable one, surprising, controversial, funny, tragic. Nor has it been told before.

Few mammals have been so negatively named. In 1803, when a ragged boatload of English officers, sailors and convicts settled on the banks of the broad Derwent River, deep in the south of Tasmania, they wrongly assumed the island to be a physical extension of the east coast of New Holland, the name at that time for the Australian mainland. Their mistake was understandable, for in this new place were familiar eucalypt trees, kangaroos, wallabies and parrots. The devil, however, had been extinct on the mainland for centuries and so its vocalisations were unknown to these newcomers who, lying in their tents at night, listened nervously to the beast's alien shrieks and screams emanating from densely wooded mountains and valleys.

A case can be made that the settlers heard devils before seeing them, since the animals are nocturnal and rarely about during the day. Why else christen a small, lolloping scavenger after the supreme embodiment of evil? On the other hand, there is something practical about the name. Beelzebub was Satan's first lieutenant, the prince of devils and 'lord of the flies'. Carcasses, flies and Tasmanian devils have a lot in common.

Early written reports of the animal condemned it to persecution. It was incorrectly, though perhaps understandably, described as untameably savage, highly destructive to livestock and with such a fierce bite that ordinary-sized dogs were no match for it. How to classify such a creature? The devil has had an array of taxonomic names, including the scary *Sarcophilus satanicus* (satanic meat lover) and *Diabolus ursinus* (diabolical bear). The most commonly accepted name is *Sarcophilus harrisii*, after the Deputy Surveyor General George Harris who in 1806 described and sketched the devil for the London Zoological Society. But some scientists have in recent times opted for *S. laniarius*, after mainland fossils so named in the 1830s by the French naturalists Georges Cuvier and Geoffroy Saint-Hilaire, and the English palaeontologist Richard Owen. To add to the uncertainty, there is also *S. moornaensis*, an even earlier mainland fossil, as well as another possible species nestled in time and size between *S. moornaensis* and the extant species.[2] On the other hand, in good Australian vernacular the devil might well be called the pied jumbuck-gobbler, *Gulpemdownus woollyturdii*.

In 1830 the devil was singled out, along with the thylacine, as stock-destroying vermin to be eliminated through bounty schemes. Yet neither of these species was to blame for livestock losses, as shown by 80 years of bounty records painstakingly collected by Eric Guiler. The real culprits in the hard early years of the colony of Van Diemen's Land were poor management decisions and practices, and large packs of feral dogs. It has to be said, though, that the sight of a few devils tearing into a cast

Tasmanian bush myths perpetuate an incorrect fear that devils will attack and eat wounded or incapacitated bushwalkers. No such attack has ever been recorded. (Courtesy Nick Mooney)

sheep or sick lamb does leave a strong impression.

And what of Packer's fear on Boviak Beach? It is true that devils will eat people, but only cadavers and only if the opportunity is there, such as finding a suicide or murder victim in the bush. Tasmania Police forensic services invariably call upon Nature Conservation Branch officers Nick Mooney and Mark Holdsworth on such occasions.

There are, needless to say, Tasmanian devil bush myths, such as the couple hiking in the wilderness: one slips and becomes trapped under a fallen log, the other goes to get help, returns the next morning, and . . . only femur bones and boot-soles are left. In another, a drunk falls into a cattle trough and drowns with his arm hanging out, which gets eaten off.

But an element of caution is probably no bad thing. Alan Scott is manager of the Cameron family farm 'Kingston', at the foot of Ben Lomond. He describes the sprawling property as being 'in the middle of nowhere'.[3] (The late Major R. Cameron swore that in 1998 he saw a pair of thylacines on the property.) Scott says of the disease—that has struck hard in the region—that it is terrible no longer having devils about the place. Yet when he first began working on the property many years ago, and was required to do lone mustering on horseback in remote back paddocks, he feared the prospect of taking a fall, of being incapacitated far from help with night coming on. Indeed, Mooney says he has come across this fear many times.

Devils are opportunistic feeders, not specialist predators. They eat a variety of foods. They do kill live prey, and they forage for carrion, both vertebrate and invertebrate. While there are a few, unsubstantiated, reports of cooperative hunting, with one devil flushing prey and the other chasing it down, the animal is overwhelmingly a solitary hunter. The devil's physique, stealth and ability to run quickly in short bursts make it a good night hunter, with wombats favoured for their fat content and their relative slowness. A devil is incapable of running down a bounding wallaby or sprinting rabbit. Its jaw strength and teeth have evolved to consume carrion, including tough gristle, skin and large bones.

Technically, if a sick lamb or wallaby is near death and a devil begins to eat it, that is an act of predation, not foraging, despite the devil having no role in bringing its 'prey' to that state. It is also technically correct to state that devils hunt tadpoles and moths, both of which feature in their diet. And if a devil opportunistically scents a nest of helpless baby quolls, native hens,

wombats or, indeed, devils, and consumes them, that is predation, although the behaviour associated with the act is foraging.

That the devil is not a selective or timid eater is amply borne
out, and not just by the antics of its tree-and-rock-chomping
cartoon counterpart (which Warner Bros. brought to life in 1954
when there was hardly any available literature on devil behaviour). Items such as shoes regularly disappear off the verandahs of
beach shacks and, if ever found again, have been well chewed.
Devils love scavenging around rubbish dumps, but so do other
opportunistic carnivores such as spotted-tailed quolls, cats,
bears, hyaenas and foxes. Devils frequent beaches in search of
dead fish and much else potentially edible deposited on the
tideline. On one occasion at Geoff King's 'devil restaurant',
during the day, Nick Mooney watched newly independent devils
fossicking for and eating kelp maggots.

David Randall, who worked as a ranger for many years in all
parts of Tasmania, studied the native water rats of the Freycinet
Peninsula on the east coast by trapping them with chunks of
possum. One morning he found a sprung trap that a devil had
subsequently broken into, forcing the wire apart to get at the
bait and whatever creature was in there with it.

Garry Sutton, ranger in charge of the Narawntapu National
Park in northern Tasmania, once had to shoot an injured horse in
the park. Because of its size and the park's public role, he used a
front-end loader to dig a deep hole and bury the animal. Devils
soon dug tunnels down through the sand to the decomposing
corpse.

One of Alan Scott's cows died giving birth. He left the corpse
overnight and returned the next morning to see 'a devil coming
out the backside'.[4] That's not unusual: the easiest way into a

Staked out roadkill wallabies provide the bill of fare attracting devils to the island's scattering of devil restaurants. (Courtesy Nick Mooney)

large animal is through the soft parts. And Guiler reported that he and a colleague 'found three devils sleeping off their feast inside the rib cage of a cow they were consuming'.[5]

The observed record for devils feeding simultaneously—also on a cow—is 22. This is a remarkable behavioural aspect of this generally solitary animal. It is also misunderstood behaviour, and one of the reasons why devils have such a bad reputation.

Far from being a free-for-all, communal devil feeding is structured and purposeful, and is properly described as ritualised behaviour. The screaming and apparent fighting is an elaborate combination and variety of vocalisations and postures by which order is maintained. The noises also act as a compass at night, alerting other devils in the area—just as daylight-circling vultures attract others—which saves them wasting energy looking for food. Smaller carcasses equal less noise. The perceived practice of eating 'everything'—because it disappears—is the result of individuals taking what they can and hiding with their share to consume it in peace.

Devils are the great hygienists of the Tasmanian bush and long ago extended that courtesy to farmers, eating their dead and sick livestock and in the process breaking the sheep tapeworm cycle, keeping the blowfly population down and relieving conscientious landowners of the need to bury dead stock. For these reasons there have been proposals to introduce devils to Flinders Island and King Island, where roadkill wildlife smells and is unsightly, attracting adverse reactions from tourists. One problem with the proposal is that the same danger would be posed to devils feeding by the roadside: speeding cars. A solution would be to heave roadkill into the bush, where it can be consumed in safety. Devil researcher Menna Jones and her volunteers did this along the road to Coles Bay on the Freycinet Peninsula almost every night during the years of her work there. The number of devils killed by cars decreased dramatically.

Communal feeding gives rise to the apparent paradox that this asocial animal indulges in a complex social ritual as often as every third or fourth night. David Parer, an internationally known film-maker specialising in wildlife documentaries, has spent many years filming and observing devils and is well aware of the social nature of the species: 'We think of them as bad-tempered and vicious but watch them in the den and their family lives are not unlike a human life. There's playtime, squabbles, dinner time, discipline problems, teaching and learning'.[6]

Are Tasmanian devils dangerous? Of the many people working closely with devils—biologists, orphan carers, wildlife park employees—few would disagree that although individual animals have greatly varying personalities the species as a whole is timid. A wild devil trapped in a cage (though not a painful leg-hold trap or snare) will 'freeze' or become inert and won't struggle if carefully handled. Quolls, by contrast, bolt as soon as they can, and possums are notoriously difficult to handle. Guiler experimented empirically by putting devils and rats together in a small enclosure. The devils, he reported, were at times wary of the scurrying rats. If anyone knew them, Guiler did: 'most of the more than 7000 Tasmanian devils he handled were docile to the point of being lethargic and could be handled with ease'.[7]

On the other hand devil rage, though rare, is real. Early in 2005 two wildlife volunteers released a newly weaned devil from a trap. It turned and chased them so aggressively that they had to leap onto their car. Devils can often be seen chasing one another in their wildlife park enclosures, and the same behaviour occurs in the wild during feeding bouts.

Devils scare easily and when startled will often shake. A screeching and biting devil acting purely out of fear will, however, if held firmly, become very still. And they are sensitive. In 2004 both David Pemberton and his family and Nick and Kate Mooney hand-reared devils whose mothers had died from DFTD. Pemberton visited the Mooneys one Saturday, after which, said Nick, their devil Eric, 'a charismatic charmer with a short fuse, came in behaving normally, until Kate fired up the vacuum cleaner—he changed completely and has remained one hundred per cent timid for days, hiding in dark corners. I suspect a combination of [lingering] smells from David's devils [on his clothes] and the size and noise of the cleaner may have told him that a large, dominant devil had entered the house'.[8]

Juvenile devils display some of the characteristics of young domestic animals— inquisitiveness, playfulness. (Courtesy David Pemberton)

Timid and sensitive, yes—yet in the popular imagination the devil has always been considered quite the opposite, as in this ludicrous 1917 description:

> Curiosity having been aroused as to why these ugly things received their highly suggestive name, it was stated that there can be little doubt that they deserved it. It is another case of ugliness going to the bone. Indeed, any virtues they possess are negative ones, and their vices are most positive. They are very savage, and have frequent fights among themselves, while they slay other creatures for the mere wanton lust of slaughter. When they attack anything, a member of their own tribe or any other species, they will practically tear it to pieces in sheer ruthlessness . . . During the day it is too sleepy to be otherwise than very stupid, but with the oncoming of covering darkness it displays a cunning and a cleverness inseparably connected in the human mind with the original owners of the despised name of devil.[9]

Or this:

> The Tasmanian Devil (*Sarcophilus ursinus*) has the reputation of
> being the fiercest, most wantonly destructive beast in the
> animal kingdom. It is ugly and morose; a small animal, black
> with a white front to the throat, it is capable of doing enormous
> damage to sheep, killing wantonly sometimes large numbers of
> the flocks. Fortunately for the Tasmanian farmer, if not for
> Natural History, the number of devils is decreasing rapidly.[10]

No less a scientist than Clive Lord, an eminent early Director of
the Tasmanian Museum and Art Gallery, described the devil as
'exceedingly quarrelsome'[11] and later as 'of fierce disposition . . . It
cannot be considered a pleasant animal to have much to do with'.[12]

*Errors of fact by professionals haven't helped the devil. This watercolour is by
D. Colbron Pearse, who for a period in the 1950s was acting Director of the
Tasmanian Museum and Art Gallery. The young are not accurate depictions of
devils—rather, they are hybrids of spotted-tailed quolls and devils.
(Courtesy Collection Tasmanian Museum and Art Gallery)*

Devils were presumed to be scarce when Lord wrote about them and, if they were, it is possible that he had relied on scanty and biased rural accounts for his observations, because he was wrong on all three counts.

Mistakes are understandable—up to a point. When, in 1962, a London newspaper ran a feature on Tasmanian devils and accompanied it with a photograph of a thylacine, the editor received fourteen complaints.[13] Less forgivable is a popular American animal encyclopedia which, even in its sixth printing in 1988, stated: 'The Tasmanian devil is jet black with white blotches and a bright pink nose, ears, feet and tail . . . The Devil is a burrower but when cornered it will often dive into the water and swim a long distance before surfacing under banks or overhanging vegetation'.[14] As a combination of a platypus and a kindergarten painting this takes some beating.

Equally improbable is the link the Tasmanian devil supposedly had with the enduring American myth of the Jersey Devil. This creature allegedly came to exist in the eighteenth century in the swamps of south-eastern New Jersey, having a horse-like head, wings, cloven feet and thick tail. Sightings of it were regular, including one by Napoleon Bonaparte's brother Joseph while hunting there (Joseph lived in America between 1815 and 1832) and it was even seen in the company of a headless pirate. Joseph Bonaparte may have known of a strange new 'devil' animal because his sister-in-law, the Empress Josephine, kept a menagerie that included marsupials.

During one week in 1909, some 30 sightings of the Jersey Devil caused near-panic. The Smithsonian Institution speculated that it might be a Jurassic survivor, possibly a pterodactyl or peleosaurus which had survived in the region's limestone caves.

More plausible, if that is the word, was that 'New York scientists thought it to be a marsupial carnivore'.[15]

But confusion arising out of words and myth pales beside reality on the ground. Tasmanian devils have been mercilessly persecuted. Nineteenth-century bounty hunting gave way to widespread strychnine poisoning in the early and middle decades of the twentieth century, with baits laid by farmers and also by trappers who made a living from possum and wallaby pelts. Snaring was a substantial business; in the 1923 season, for instance, 693 147 possums were snared and about half that number of wallabies.[16] Yet spotted-tailed quolls probably damaged more snared animals than devils did, because they had a greater ability to reach a carcass suspended above the ground.

Likewise poorly attached chicken wire won't protect poultry from hungry devils, but their disappearance from many rural areas has not meant that hens are now safe. Max Cameron, the owner of 'Kingston', bought twelve hens for a new property near Trowunna and put them in a sealed room overnight. A quoll got into the room through a drain and 'necked'—killed and blood-sucked—all of them.[17]

Yet the Tasmanian devil has been an easy target for so long that, like the ethereal Jersey Devil flying through the mists of its densely wooded swamps, truth and reality are secondary to established myth.

Devils can stink—if they have been in a trap or cage for an extended period and their coats become matted with excrement. Adults have a naturally musty, waxy odour, but young devils are as clean-smelling as puppies and kittens. The perception that the animals stink because they eat rotting meat is incorrect, and reflects a lack of first-hand experience.

Their famed jaw strength is very real—the equivalent of that of a dog four times their size, or, for their body mass, more powerful than a tiger's. The earliest steel wire traps used by Guiler proved useless, since some adult devils were able to chew their way through the thick wire. When trapping devils in the 1950s naturalist David Fleay was astounded to find a devil wearing a glistening yellow metal 'collar', until he recalled that two weeks previously a special composite foot-snare of brass wire and hemp set for a thylacine had been found sprung and bitten off.[18] Even so, devils are incapable of chewing through the biggest bones of large animals. And tough hide is very difficult to chew and ingest. Thus while wombat flesh and the prized fat is devoured, devils generally leave the backbone and adjoining skin of these rugged herbivores.

The devil's range of vocalisations is truly impressive. There are at least eleven distinct vocalisations, but describing them isn't easy. Writing in 1806, Harris described 'a sudden kind of snorting'.[19] One hundred and fifty years later Fleay heard that sound as 'wheezing coughs that sounded harshly like "Horace"',[20] while for the excitable *Reminiscences From the Melbourne Zoo* correspondent:

> If one could imagine a choir consisting of imps in the infernal regions, with every ear-splitting, brain-scratching sound grouped in hideous discords, the only earthly model that could be used as a guide would be a chorus from a company of Tasmanian devils.[21]

According to German conservationist Bernhard Grzimek:

> The Tasmanian devil which lived with us at Frankfurt Zoo for a number of years used to sing loudly and persistently when

encouraged to. When cleaning out its cage, all we had to do was to stand in front of it and give the right note, and the animal would open its mouth and join in, keeping up the performance for quite a while. (I had earlier managed to get my wolves to sing in the same way.)[22]

Director of the Frankfurt Zoo, Grzimek devoted himself to wildlife conservation, particularly in Tanzania, and his influential 1959 documentary *Serengeti Shall Not Die* won an Oscar award. Eric Guiler also 'sang' with a number of the devils he kept at the University of Tasmania.

Mary Roberts owned Beaumaris Zoo in Hobart early in the twentieth century. She particularly loved devils and developed a close relationship with them; they eagerly responded to her calls.

It is not a myth that devils like water. Captive devils regularly splash around in their water pools and clearly enjoy it. On his trapping expedition Fleay witnessed a not uncommon sight: 'Another huge fellow . . . glared balefully from behind a shut [trap] door one morning and when I turned him loose he rushed for the river bank, dived into the icy current and swam strongly to the opposite side disappearing among the ferns'.[23] Nick Mooney has seen a devil swim powerfully across the fast-flowing, 50-metre wide Arthur River.

Their speed on land has not been fully appreciated. The general perception is that, because they are short-legged and have an awkward-looking gait, they are incapable of running quickly. Guiler seemed to confirm this. 'It lopes along at about 3–4 kilometres per hour, but when chased it can make about 12 kilometres per hour for a short time. Several times we have caught devils by running after them when they have escaped while being handled.'[24]

Others have different opinions. David Randall and a wildlife officer friend, Reuben Hooper, were discussing the extent to which the devil could be an efficient chase-and-catch predator. They decided upon an empirical test. Randall released a devil which Hooper chased. The devil outsprinted Hooper, then suddenly stopped, turned and hissed at him, and he had to leap over it.

Artist and naturalist George Davis has had a lifelong interest in Tasmania's flora and wildlife. He believes that in their wild state, with no roadkill or livestock, devils have no choice but to hunt and catch, and he can testify to their fleetness of foot—he once chased one in a Land Rover. The Tasmanian Government's environment website states that devils have been clocked running on a flat road at 25 kmh for up to 1.5 kilometres,[25] and at Cradle Mountain Menna Jones clocked one running in her headlights at 35 kmh for 300 metres.

What is certain is that devils have great stamina. David Pemberton's fieldwork in the 1980s involved radio-tracking individuals throughout the night. A typical pattern emerged: an animal leaves its den after dark and, at a steady lope, uses tracks and forest edges to investigate known food-source areas. Bursts of speed are intermingled with periods of stillness, lasting up to half an hour. That pattern suggests an ambush predator. Towards the end of the night the devil sets up a rapid nonstop lope to return to its den around dawn. Its ability to travel a long way, at a good pace and quietly, is impressive and is a typical attribute of the polyphagous carnivores—those which according to dictionaries have an 'excessive' desire to eat. Devil speeds of greater than 10 kmh are common for extended periods through the night, three or four times per week.

A famed devil story that happens to be true relates to sheep in shearing sheds, and the problem likely to beset one if a leg slips through the flooring slats and becomes stuck. Lionel Grey, a cull shooter, says he has come across a sheep in a shed 'with the hock chewed off it'[26], as has Helen Gee, who farms at Buckland. Sceptics wonder if this is another farmers' myth to tarnish the devil, asking why sheep would be left overnight in a shearing shed. But they frequently are, being penned overnight for an early start in the morning. And because many farms have been cleared of even small stands of timber, devils perforce set up dens under buildings, including shearing sheds.

Older Tasmanian houses sometimes have devil dens in their foundations, having possibly been in use for more than a hundred years, with no one being aware of their presence, though smell and noise are usually the giveaway. Nick Mooney is often called to remove devils from under houses. His preferred method is to install a one-way cat flap at the den entrance once any juveniles are large enough that they are naturally emerging and using other, secondary dens.

He has had a few memorable den experiences. One couple reported devil pups under their house and wanted to know if they could be shifted. Mooney talked them out of it for that season. The husband was a school soccer coach and after one match he brought two teams' jumpers home to wash. He left them in a bag on the verandah overnight and they subsequently disappeared. He assumed they had been stolen. Mooney reckoned otherwise. Knowing where the devils were denned, under the kitchen floor, he popped a plank—and there were the jumpers. He recollects that they fished up about 30 using a wire. None had been chewed and after being washed were fine. They retrieved a number of other items as well, including a pillow.

At another house, a litter of young devils was attracted to a feather-filled doona being aired on a clothesline. They pulled it off the line and tried to drag it through a hole into the house's foundations. They managed to get most of it in before it burst, showering the foundations with feathers. Mooney recalls wet black noses with white feathers stuck on them, and plenty of devil sneezing. He bought the owner a new doona.

During 2004, David Pemberton and his partner Rosemary Gales hand-reared two devils, Donny and Clyde, who made their den under a bed in a spare room. They regularly took items of newly washed clothing to the den. By the time Donny and Clyde were moved to the wild, they had lined their den with the equivalent of three basket-loads of clean washing.

A fact that could be mistaken for a myth is the tendency of devils to all go to the toilet in the same spot. The use of communal latrines is not common among animals. Hyaenas and ratels (honey badgers), two other species associated with the devil through convergent evolution, also use communal latrines. They are instances of an apparently solitary animal engaging in at least chemical social interaction. Depending on population numbers, dozens of devils will defecate in one area—usually near a creek crossing or other water source—for reasons of communication barely understood, and further calling into question the 'solitary' tag. The same spot will be reused by a devil after an absence of a week or more, which implies a form of territoriality. Devil latrines could be described as community noticeboards; they may tell transients that a particular area is full, and they may tell competing males something about female availability. They may even have an inter-species communication function: spotted-tailed quoll scats have been found at devil latrines.

Nick and Kate Mooney have hand-reared many orphaned devils for rehabilitation and have little difficulty toilet-training them because of the innate behavioural tendency to use one latrine.

Devil scats are huge and in them, as befits an unfussy feeder, are to be found a great variety of objects. So big are they relative to the animal's size that they have often been cited as evidence of the continued existence of thylacines. An average scat is about 15 centimetres long, but they can be up to 25 centimetres long.

Baby and juvenile devils are cute, playful, mischievous—and noisy, especially during the night. They climb whatever they can and play games which involve ambushing, chasing and dragging one another by the ear. David Pemberton, while rearing orphans, has observed that juvenile devils use their tails to send a range of excitable and nervous signals, with the tail bent stiffly toward the ground and twitching energetically. (Raised tails in most animals are generally considered the demonstration of a highly excitable state.)

Yet devils would not make good pets. Even little ones have formidably sharp teeth and vice-like jaws. Above all, once weaned they become asocial, which is surely why Aborigines, who quickly took to dogs after European settlement, did not keep them as pets. This hasn't prevented some Australian scientists suggesting that endangered marsupials be tested as pets, with a view to breeding them up. A report on ABC Radio's *PM* program began with host Mark Colvin introducing the topic this way: 'Imagine curling up in front of a winter fire with a Tasmanian devil at your feet, or an eastern quoll on your lap . . .'[27] Having said this hand-reared devils do like their comfort— some of the Mooneys' winter orphans would gather at the fire-place and wait for the fire to be lit.

Their protected status has not prevented a number of US exotic pet websites advertising devils. The international trade in exotic living things is vast and much of it illegal. It would be surprising if devils didn't form part of it, because they would sell handsomely, thanks in part to the high profile of the Warner Bros. cartoon character Taz. They are easy to catch, feed and house. But Tasmania's rural population is small and interconnected and locals involved in such a trade would have to go about their cruel business with great caution.

An incident in Perth, Western Australia, in July 1997 appears to confirm that there is such a trade. As reported by CNN, a woman found:

> an unusual illegal immigrant hiding under her car: a
> Tasmanian Devil . . . The Department of Conservation and
> Land Management did a little checking around. There are 16
> registered licensees in Western Australia who are permitted to
> keep Tasmanian Devils, and none of them was missing any.
> The department believes the animal was imported illegally and
> kept as a pet before escaping.[28]

US Navy aircraft carriers occasionally visit Hobart, and in one year in the 1990s strong rumours were about that a number of sailors with Tasmanian devil tattoos—the animal was their group mascot—swapped or attempted to swap handguns for live devils.

Devil experts are occasionally asked if the animals can interbreed with dogs, the unspoken reason being a desire to breed a presumably omnipotent fighting hound.

Cruelty and ignorance have hurt the devil in many ways. One or two individual farmers are believed to have had an annual kill rate of over 1000 a year, through strychnine poisoning, trained dogs and mass trapping. George Davis witnessed a particularly cruel method of killing them. A northern farmer placed a 220-litre water tank in the ground and ran a baited drop-plank over it, luring devils onto the plank which then tipped them into the tank, where they fought and ate one another.

An east coast farmer used to kill them by nailing a baited shark hook to a tree trunk, at a height that would hook the devil on tiptoes so that it couldn't escape and would die in agony. A head keeper at Bonorong Wildlife Park witnessed fifteen shot devils being thrown on a bonfire. A senior Parks and Wildlife officer was heard to say that while he would avoid a wombat on the road, devils were fair game.

In 1993 Mooney found 32 dead devils around poisoned sheep carcasses, near a popular trout fishing spot in the central highlands. All had had their saddles skinned off. It appeared to be a mass killing for perhaps a floor mat, and such a mat may well adorn a central highlands fishing shack.

In 1952 David Fleay wrote:

> Fur trappers who still carry on large scale operations during the winters of western Tasmania heartily dislike the snare-despoiling Devil, and often go to extreme lengths to rid a particular area of these animals before the season begins. An old pine shack below the frowning Frenchman Range is still known as the Devil's Camp—thanks to the pitiless work carried out by the first snarers there who poisoned and trapped the unfortunate carnivores so that their whitened bones lay in that vicinity for many years afterwards.[29]

The apparent capacity of the devil to survive in both 'plague' and dangerously low numbers, despite human interference, seems to be another of its remarkable features, but to believe so is to perpetuate the myth that the natural world, like an ageless superheavyweight boxer, can continue to absorb everything thrown at it. And it may be that a combination of human-induced factors is fully or partly responsible for the outbreak of the devastating DFTD, from which the devil may not recover. Little is yet known about the disease beyond the fact that it spreads through populations and kills individual animals within about six months. Half of Tasmania was affected by the beginning of 2005. There is no historical account of a devil with gross external tumours, which indicates that DFTD could be a 'new' disease and thus may be associated with human activity. An early twentieth-century decline—if it did happen—is more likely to have been linked to thylacine trapping and the snaring of possums and wallabies than to disease.

Can devil numbers sustain 'everything'? The question hinges at least in part on 'numbers'. Despite decades of research, devil

Devils don't always benefit from food provided by roadkill. (Courtesy Nick Mooney)

population shifts defy easy explanation. George Davis recalls that, as a boy in Pelham during the early 1940s, the capture of a devil caused excitement because the creature was so rare. David Randall remembers them being very uncommon everywhere in the 1950s, and also in low numbers in the late 1960s. Yet by the early 1970s and again in the late 1980s, farmers in the east and northeast complained of 'plague numbers' threatening the sheep industry.

Interference with food supply may affect devils. Davis recalls night shoots when a bag of three or four wallabies was considered good. The introduction of spotlight shooting in the late 1960s, at the same time as a great increase in the amount of agricultural browsing land, meant that suddenly hundreds of carcasses were being dumped every night. More food meant more devils, and consequently a human-induced alteration to natural population dynamics.

Roads might be another influence on devils where roadkills are common, for instance near barley fields which are particularly attractive to wallabies. Do devils live in greater numbers near roads which offer up a steady supply of roadkill? It is impossible to know what influence human factors have on devil movements and especially their den sites, which are the critical factors in the home range location. If, over time, human activities have disrupted naturally occurring devil genetic dispersal patterns, the final outcome may be population chaos followed by extinction.

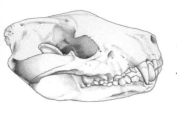

2 EVOLUTION AND EXTINCTION

Late into the night with our little boat anchored just outside the weedline about thirty metres from shore we heard an ungodly commotion. Spotlight quickly activated to find a Tasmanian devil tearing open the tightly wrapped package of sandwiches which it had somehow managed to get out of an airtight lunch box. In the couple of minutes it took to start the outboard motor and push the boat through the weeds to shore the devil and complete contents of the lunch box were gone. The devil had obviously eaten in silence until it got to the sandwiches. It must have got frustrated with the plastic wrap hence the sudden noisy outburst.

BRIAN GEORGE, SORELL

Long ago, in the Dreamtime, deep in the Tasmanian bush, Wing-go-wing the Tasmanian devil finished eating her dinner. She didn't, though, have a full stomach and was still hungry. She started hunting again and spied a kangaroo. 'This would taste just right and fill up the hollow in my stomach,' she said. Ooroo, the kangaroo, didn't see Wing-go-wing approaching . . . creeping . . . unseen. Wing-go-wing chased after Ooroo, snapping at its legs. He bounded off as fast as he could, but Wing-go-wing caught hold of Ooroo. Wing-go-wing bit off the bottom of Ooroo's legs and the end of his tail. Ooroo, though, escaped and bounced into the thick scrub. Wing-go-wing was happy with this little snack and quickly ate what she caught. Ooroo, the now much shorter kangaroo, turned into a pademelon. The pademelon has short legs and a short tail. The pademelon is now always careful of Tasmanian devils and, to this day, wishes it had its longer legs and its longer tail. Wing-go-wing finished her kangaroo nibble but was still hungry. She thought possum would taste nice for dessert. Be-U, the possum, sat in his tree having witnessed what had just happened to Ooroo and he thought he would teach this Tasmanian devil a lesson. Be-U hid behind a stump of an old tree. Wing-go-wing approached, sniffing for possum. Be-U jumped out, holding a sharp stick in one of his paws. He struck Wing-go-wing across the neck and the devil screamed loudly. Be-U, with his other paw, threw white sand at Wing-go-wing and it stuck in the cut. Some of the sand went into Wing-go-wing's mouth. Be-U scrambled up a tree to see Wing-go-wing below. The devil's throat was now as white as Mount Wellington snow. From now on other bush animals could see the devil coming before Wing-go-wing could bite them. Wing-go-wing screamed at Be-U. The devil's voice, though, was now harsh and gravely. The sand had changed the devil's noise. The other bush animals would hear her coming and know to run away before it was too late. Be-U, hanging by his tail, laughed at Wing-go-wing, and was very happy that he could help his bush friends. But he knew he would always have to be watchful, especially at night, of Tasmanian devils who were hungry . . . and angry . . .[1]

The Tasmanian devil has the distinction of being the world's largest living marsupial carnivore, though since an adult male devil seldom weighs more than 12 kilograms the species cannot be compared with dominant placental carnivores in other parts of the world, such as lions, tigers and wolves. Many factors, operating across millions of years, have resulted in the devil occupying this unique position.

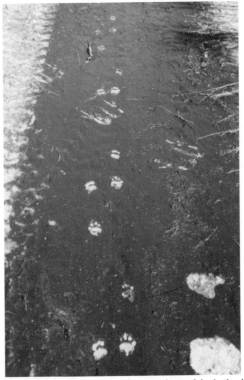

These prints on an iced-over creek demonstrate the unusual gait of the devil, which may have descended from an arboreal ancestor that hopped along branches. (Courtesy Nick Mooney)

Australia once formed part of the southern hemisphere super-continent of Gondwana, together with what would become South America, Antarctica, Madagascar, New Zealand, India and Africa. While it is not known precisely how Australia's marsupials evolved, fragmentary fossil evidence suggests that lineages of protomarsupial stocks originating in South America journeyed across the then-temperate Antarctic landmass. Australia became a continent about 45 million years ago, floating free with a cargo of flora and fauna that would evolve in isolation until the continent collided with the Indonesian archipelago. That isolation enabled marsupials to diversify free of competition, but the 'floating laboratory' created competition of another kind, in the form of major climate changes brought about by variation in global weather patterns, Australia's northward movement towards the equator, and the southern hemisphere ocean, wind and pressure changes created by that movement. Enormous inland seas and tropical forests came and went, periodically giving way to colder, drier conditions.

Although the continent had at times supported big mountain ranges, its general overall flatness provided little protection from the subantarctic winds that scoured away much of its surface. The remaining nutrient-poor soils, increasing surface salinity, decreasing rainfall, and extreme fluctuations between day-time heat and night-time cold, determined the long-term evolution of unique, often sparse, tree, plant and grass forms. Australia's herbivores developed accordingly. They became either nocturnal or crepuscular (active at dawn and dusk) browsers and grazers. There were none of the vast herds of grazing animals that developed on the lush grasslands of Africa and North America, for example, so there was limited scope for predators.

The devil's unknown ancestors may well have been tree-dwellers, eating insects, nectar, fruits and young leaves. As those creatures grew larger, their hind legs may have begun to operate in unison to cope with moving along branches, leading eventually to the hopping gait that is characteristic of many marsupials. This may even explain the devil's unusual gait.

The devil's specific lineage appears to be a result of dramatic climate change around the middle of the Miocene Epoch (16 million–5 million years ago). Australia had experienced a long period of warm, moist conditions. Inland seas and rivers dominated the continent and supported a great variety of animal, bird and aquatic life. Not surprisingly, many types of predators flourished in that period. But the rapid onset of the first of many ice ages changed that. Colder, drier conditions shrank the forests until, 'at its peak, far more than half of the continent became technically arid'.[2] Major extinctions resulted.

A few carnivores survived. Two were ancestors of the thylacine and the quoll genus, both of them hunters. It may be that specialist scavenging came to be an important niche, with the thylacine in particular ensuring a supply of carrion through its habit of selective feeding. This may be how the devil line arose. The species has no known earlier ancestry, unlike both the thylacine and quoll, which trace back at least 25 million years. The extinct species *Glaucodon ballaratensis* from the Pliocene (around 5 million–2 million years ago) is described as an 'intermediate form' between quoll and devil.[3] Although this suggests evolutionary experimentation in response to the increasingly dry environment, speculation based on fragmentary fossil evidence must be treated with care.

Australia's Miocene fossil record was considered poor until, in the early 1980s, the rich Riversleigh fossil deposits in north-western Queensland were properly surveyed. At some 100 sites, huge numbers of limestone-encased fossils are preserved in ancient cave systems and waterways. 'Almost half of what we know about the evolution of Australian mammals in the last 30 million years comes from bones found at a single site in the Riversleigh fossil beds. Half of that was unearthed in one hour.'[4]

Riversleigh was granted World Heritage status, together with the much younger limestone fossil sites at Naracoorte Caves, in southeastern South Australia. There the devil is represented in the extraordinarily rich Fossil Chamber, a huge cave into which animals fell over a period of some 300 000 years, creating a gigantic cone of well-preserved bone deposits. Although Naracoorte and Riversleigh contain a wealth of information yet to be tapped, they have enabled a vivid reconstruction of Australia's relatively recent but mysterious age of marsupial megafauna.

These giant creatures established themselves as the continent became colder and more arid. They dominated during the most recent Ice Age into the Pleistocene Epoch but were then subject to rapid mass extinction, a process that began about 70 000 years ago and ended when the last of them died away about 20 000 years ago, though these time-spans are as controversial as the reasons put forward to explain the extinctions.

Sarcophilus laniarius is the devil species found in the Naracoorte Fossil Chamber. It was about 15 per cent larger than a modern devil, making its body mass about 50 per cent greater. But caution is necessary. 'The relationships between the living Tasmanian Devil and the larger Pleistocene form are in doubt . . . The living animal may either be a dwarfed version of *S. laniarius* or possibly a different species that coexisted with the latter.'[5] It was the eminent nineteenth-century palaeontologist Richard Owen (who discovered and classified *S. laniarius*) who originally proposed the idea of different coexisting sizes, based on fossils discovered in the Wellington caves of New South Wales in 1877.

Giant devil bones have also been found in Queensland, Western Australia, New South Wales and Tasmania. The earliest fossil evidence is from the Fishermans Cliff locality in south-western New South Wales, where the species is described as *S. moornaensis*. The first appearances of *S. laniarius* are in a fossil deposit in the eastern Darling Downs of southeastern Queensland, and in the Victoria Cave deposit in South Australia. Dating these sites is difficult, but the species certainly was present between 70 000 and 50 000 years ago. The Mammoth Cave site in Western Australia, where *S. laniarius* has also been found, may be as old as 70 000 years. The Devil's Lair cave deposit in Western Australia is dated at 11 000 to 30 000 years old and shows evidence of both devils and Aboriginal inhabitants. More recent deposits from the Holocene Epoch (the past 10 000–11 000 years) are found throughout Australia, including on Flinders Island in Bass Strait.

A fragment of a megafaunal devil jaw in the Queen Victoria Museum and Art Gallery in Launceston is about 50 per cent larger than that of the extant species. It would no doubt have been a most efficient carrion eater because, like the present-day devil, it was designed to consume most parts of a carcass including bones.

It is also possible that the giant devil was a hunter as well as a scavenger. Another such hunter was *Megalania prisca* (ancient giant butcher), an enormous hunting goanna five or more metres long:

> The large skull was equipped with numerous recurved, scimitar-like teeth . . . Like its modern counterparts, *Megalania* probably scavenged from dead animals, but would have also been able to hunt and kill quite large prey . . . It would also have competed for prey with other large carnivores such as the Marsupial Lion, *Thylacoleo carnifex*.[6]

There is considerable debate about this latter statement. For a long time it was believed that *Megalania prisca*, along with the huge terrestrial crocodile *Quinkana fortirostrum* and the giant snake *Wonambi naracoortensis*, were the dominant Ice Age land predators—consigning the mammals to a lesser, inferior role. But according to University of Sydney palaeontologist Dr Stephen Wroe, 'the role of Australia's fossil reptiles has been exaggerated, while that of our marsupial carnivores has been undersold. The image of an incongruous continent dominated by reptiles in the Age of Mammals has real curiosity value, but it is a castle in the air'.[7] Wroe's assessment is based on an exhaustive re-examination of comparative weight and size estimates.

Thylacine evidence reinforces the possibility of different-sized devils coexisting as well as occupying a range of predator–scavenger niches. Seven or so genera of extinct thylacine have been discovered, dating back at least 25 million years, in a range of sizes, from that of a quoll (4 kilograms) up to about 18 kilograms. While the larger species were true hunting carnivores, the smaller species were likely to have foraged for reptiles, small mammals and insects. The relationship between devil and thylacine is close enough to infer similar evolutionary traits in the challenging Australian environment.

The demise of the megafauna was both swift and extensive: virtually everything in excess of about 40 kilograms became extinct. This meant more than 50 species. The carnivore family shrank arithmetically and literally, leaving only the devil, the quolls and a single thylacine species representing medium- to large-sized mammal predators. Indeed, all modern Australian marsupials are true survivors, reflecting 'the considerable evolutionary fine-tuning that has allowed them to cope with the drastically altered climates and escalating environmental stress of the last five million years'.[8] But was there something other than smaller size that spared them from the fate of the megafauna? Climate change, human influence, or a combination of the two, have all been proposed as the agent of the antipodean mass extinction.

Climate proponents argue that at the height of the most recent Ice Age, between 18 000 and 22 000 years ago, the Australian environment had become incapable of sustaining large herbivores. Their world shifted from being cold and dry to warm and dry; the bigger the animal, the less adaptable it was to rapid environmental change. Over a relatively short period of time, Australia's preponderance of rainforest gave way to open woodland, then to savannah, then to desert. Food and water ran out for all but the smaller, more robust creatures, and for some reason there was a fairly specific cut-off body size.

In the absence of irrefutable evidence, can the climate theory be tested? Modern Australia has long been under the influence of the so-called ENSO effect, being the combined influence of El Niño and the Southern Oscillation, the former disrupting the regular rainfall patterns of the latter through cooling of the upper layer of the southern Pacific Ocean. The result across eastern Australia in particular is drought, sustained over perhaps five years before returning warm sea currents create heavy rains and floods. It's unpredictable and harsh, and the continent's arid-adapted wildlife reflects that. But there are a few exceptions. The Daintree tropical rainforest system in far northeast Queensland supports abundant and complex populations of flora and fauna, while Tasmania, a significant area of which is Gondwanan remnant forest, supported the carnivorous devil, thylacine and eastern quoll after their mainland extinctions.

Proponents of the human interference theory believe that migrating waves of people slaughtered the megafauna to such an extent that they became extinct. This would have to have taken place well before the peak in late Ice Age climate aridity (to disprove climate as the culprit), and suggestions are that the megafauna began to be slaughtered about 46 000 years ago. This so-called Blitzkrieg hypothesis infers swift and rampant overkilling, as seemingly happened with the New Zealand moas and North America's mammoths and mastodons. A less blood-thirsty explanation is that regular slaughter for consumption, together with the introduction of fire management, which significantly altered grazing and browsing habitats, induced the same extinction result but over a far longer period. In this context, Stephen Wroe contends that a significant mid-Holocene increase in human land usage could have been a primary cause.[9]

Did the devil survive because of its comparatively small size and ability to become even smaller (dwarfism)? Or was its place in the ecosystem assured because it was capable of both hunting and scavenging? Even in the absence of easy-to-catch megafauna, did people not hunt it? Why did the thylacine survive but not the larger marsupial lion?

The subsequent extinction of the devil across mainland Australia is also hard to explain. It appears the animal survived there until as recently as 500 years ago, although the introduction of dingoes some 6000 years ago is generally considered to have marked the beginning of their end. Their predator–scavenger niches overlap; dingoes will forage for young devils; and there have never been dingoes in Tasmania.

There may in addition have been a climatic factor. Devils thrive in temperate, well-covered Tasmania with its abundance of prey in a relatively compact area. Much of mainland Australia, on the other hand, has become an ever more arid and inhospitable environment since the devil survived the megafaunal

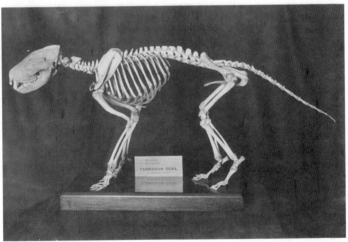

Skeleton of Sarcophilus harrisii, *the Tasmanian devil. (Courtesy Collection Tasmanian Museum and Art Gallery)*

extinction. Perhaps those conditions affected the mainland species over thousands of years until it was reduced to remnant populations in the east and southeast. Then, and only then, might the devil have succumbed to the dingo.

Megafauna-era butchering tools include scrapers of all kinds as well as axes, but it was not until some 10 000 years ago that the Aboriginal people became true hunters, with the invention of the boomerang and spear. It is suggested that prior to those technological advances, animal-taking must have been somewhat opportunistic. The famous Devil's Lair cave in south-west Western Australia, named for the extinct Tasmanian devil bones found in it, provides a clue.

Devil's Lair cave is one of the most important in Australian archaeology. By dating human occupation back some 45 000 years,[10] it confirms a much earlier human presence in the arid centre. Human markings on the walls may be the oldest on the continent. Cultural artefacts of bone and marl are also among the oldest known. Many extinct species are represented, but it appears that giant kangaroos were the primary food item, followed by wallabies and possums. If the devil was a food source, the scarcity of devil bones in the cave indicate either its rarity or a disinclination to catch and eat it. Of course, devils also live in caves.

There is, however, more recent evidence of the devil as a food source. Archaeological work at Victoria's Tower Hill Beach kitchen middens records 5000-year-old devil bones. Very few middens with devil bones have been found, but this did not stop one authority from declaring, 'the Aborigines knew how to hunt it, and they used it for food'.[11]

Writing in 1910 Fritz Noetling, Secretary of the Royal Society of Tasmania, cited a complete lack of evidence that

Tasmanian Aborigines consumed any of the marsupial predators or monotremes. 'It is undoubtedly very remarkable that even at the low state of civilisation represented by the Aborigines, human beings preferred the flesh of the herbivorous animals, and declined to eat that of the carnivorous.'[12] If this is true it may partly explain why in Tasmania devils and humans co-existed for tens of thousands of years prior to European settlement.

One of the greatest finds in Australian cultural history was made at Lake Nitchie, north of Wentworth on the Victoria–New South Wales border, in 1970. A male human skeleton, possibly 7000 years old, lay in a shallow grave. Unusually tall, he was wearing a necklace of 178 pierced Tasmanian devil teeth, collected from at least 47 animals. It has been speculated that the necklace indicates a dwindling population of *Sarcophilus*, and that it was considerably older than the skeleton. Archaeologist Josephine Flood went further: 'Indeed, if such necklaces were common, it is not surprising that Tasmanian devils became extinct'.[13] It is a startling suggestion, that the animal may have been hunted to extinction for its teeth.

On the other hand, the necklace is one of very few known to exist and required great labour to produce; this suggests it may have been of major significance. It is tantalising to speculate that the devil may therefore have held a special place in at least some societies of the distant past.

3 RELATIONSHIPS IN THE WILD

I opened the tent zip and stood scanning the area until the beam came to rest on a large full grown Tassie devil looking straight at me only ten metres away. Closer inspection revealed a shiny object (my bloody fork!) hanging out of its mouth. Since I needed that fork more than he did, I charged the devil who dropped the fork and bolted into the bush.

BRENDAN MCCROSSEN, MIENA

Tasmania's devil is twice lucky, having escaped the ancient fate of its mainland counterpart and the overt consequences of European settlement, which in a little over two hundred years has accounted for the extinction of almost half of the Australian continent's mammal species. Most infamously, the thylacine, the Tasmanian tiger, was hunted during the nineteenth century as a supposed threat to the island's sheep industry. It has not been seen for over 70 years and in 1986 was declared officially extinct. The devil has replaced the thylacine as the island's largest marsupial predator, but because devils are also reliant on scavenging,

Tasmania no longer has a specialist cursorial (free-running) native terrestrial predator.

The Tasmanian tiger, a large pursuit predator, and the Tasmanian devil, a medium-sized ambush predator and scavenger, shared more than related names: their relationship in the wild was close and complex. Devils were preyed on by thylacines, but also benefited from the uneaten parts of the thylacines' prey. Being foragers, devils undoubtedly ate denned thylacine cubs, should they come across them unprotected. As thylacines became rarer, such incidental predation may even have hastened their demise. Old thylacines encroached on the devil's niche by scavenging. There may also have been competition for dens, given the preference of both species for caves, burrows and grass sags.

Anatomically the thylacine is dog-like (a good example of convergent evolution), is considerably more streamlined than the squat, stout devil, and properly described as a cursorial predator. Yet dentition studies carried out by Menna Jones confirm that devils and thylacines competed directly, their teeth demonstrating a significant niche overlap. Although the devil is only about half the weight of a thylacine, it is by comparison heavy-bodied and, with its speed over a short distance and powerful bite and forepaw grip, capable of bringing down prey larger than itself. She cites cases of devils attacking adult wombats of up to 30 kilograms.[1] Thylacines, however, show much less tooth breakage than devils, meaning less bone-eating. Thus, while the devil 'has a highly carnivorous dentition and trophic adaptions for bone consumption . . . The thylacine groups with the canids. Their molar teeth are intermediate in grinding and slicing functions and are quite slender, with no indications of adaption for bone consumption'.[2]

The devil's comparatively greater tooth and associated jaw muscle strength leads Jones to conclude that 'the role of top predator in the Tasmanian ecosystem was, at the least, shared equally between thylacines and devils'.[3] Although the concept of 'sharing and competing' may seem to be at odds with itself, there are successful examples elsewhere. Jaguars and pumas are roughly the same size as each other, but heavy-bodied jaguars take heavy prey such as peccaries, while the lighter-built pumas prey on smaller animals such as antelope. Jones speculates that the devil may have had a slight edge over the thylacine in taking heavy wombats.

Taxonomically, devils and thylacines are not that closely related, but their similarities and their greater differences provide insight into how evolutionary fine-tuning allowed them to coexist closely. They have in common distinctive markings:

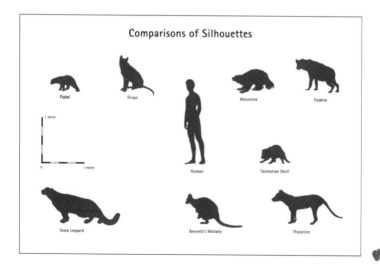

bold stripes, bold patches, which have camouflage, physiological and behavioural functions. Devil markings are important during feeding, the pure white flashes standing out at night in close interactions. The markings of both species are an indication of activity concentrated at dawn and dusk, less often during the day.

R.F. Ewer, a carnivore specialist in hyaenas and devils, speculated that a prototype/ideal canid would have both white markings and stripes to accentuate behavioural postures. While stripes aid in camouflage and possibly individual identification, white markings 'may serve to direct bites to relatively non-vulnerable areas'.[4] The thylacine has stripes, the devil has white patches. Where devil agonistic encounters result in bites they are typically on or near the rump where white markings are located (although the white chest-flash seems to play a role in initiating an encounter). Knowledge of devil marking is extremely limited. White flashes range from pronounced to marginal, with an estimated 16 per cent of animals being melanic, that is, all black.

The thick, largely non-prehensile tails of both species store fat. The devil's tail is important in physiology, locomotion and social behaviour. During high-speed motion it acts as a counter-balance.

The jaw gape of both species is wide, at 75–80 degrees, although for different reasons: thylacines used their gape to seize and suffocate or crush prey, while the gape and powerful teeth of the devil enable it to tear and gulp large lumps of food in a competitive manner, as well as to crush bones in order to consume them.

The animals' differences are pronounced. The devil's blackness is a sure asset for a small nocturnal creature; the thylacine's fawn or tan colouring shows a functional similarity to placental hunters such as wolves and wild dogs which hunt by day. An adult thylacine is about twice the weight and size of a devil. Anatomically it is considerably more streamlined than the squat, stout devil. This is because it is a cursorial predator, selecting its prey—generally a wallaby—and pursuing it relentlessly. Many early accounts refer to the thylacine's unhurried, dogged pursuit of prey, wearing its victim down through exhaustion, though it was undoubtedly capable of sharp speed over a short distance.

There was a long-held view that the thylacine was fussy and selective, consuming only the heart, kidneys and vascular tissue of its freshly killed prey, while the devil was a rapacious carrion eater. Clive Lord, director of the Tasmanian Museum in the 1920s, wrote:

> One or more Tasmanian devils will often follow a thylacine on its hunting excursions. The thylacine will kill a wallaby or other small animal, select a few choice morsels, and pass on. The devils will carry on the feast and consume the remnants, bones and all.[5]

Statements like this unwittingly consigned the two species to a strictly hierarchical relationship, and it is only in recent decades, through scientific studies, that the devil's predatory abilities have been recognised—and the likelihood that tigers and devils coexisted in a robust relationship.

Is the devil unique or can it be likened to non-marsupial mammals? Convergent evolution results when unrelated species in unrelated environments evolve similar adaptations because they occupy similar niches. Understanding and appreciation of the Tasmanian devil will be enhanced by finding convergent

Wolverines are sometimes referred to as the devil of the north. Their powerful teeth and jaws are adapted for chewing frozen carrion and crunching bone. (Courtesy Daniel J. Cox, Natural Exposures Inc.)

'relatives' elsewhere. There are three good examples: the northern hemisphere wolverine (*Gulo gulo*), the southern hemisphere ratel (*Mellivora capensis*) and the hyaenas (striped, *Hyaena hyaena*; brown, *H. brunnea*; spotted, *Crocuta crocuta*).

Wolverines and ratels belong to the Mustelidae, the weasel family, which includes weasels, minks, polecats, otters, badgers and skunks.

Historically the wolverine has a broad circumpolar range, taking in Russia, the Scandinavian countries and North America. Despite the size of its range, in the words of the Wolverine Foundation, the umbrella organisation devoted to researching and protecting it, 'Even today, the wolverine remains largely a mystery . . . one of the least understood and most fascinating creatures on earth'.[6]

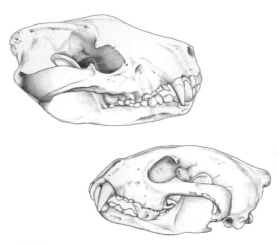

Comparative skull drawings of a Tasmanian devil (top) and a wolverine (bottom), showing the similarities of a robust carnivore skull. (Ian Faulkner)

In the United States, wolverines were once found as far south as California but appear to be confined now to Idaho and Montana, although there have been recent sightings in the Rocky Mountains states. Their Canadian range is also shrinking. The wolverine occupies a predator–scavenger niche one level down from the top predators, which in its range include wolves, bears, mountain lions and lynxes. This is not dissimilar to the Tasmanian devil–thylacine relationship.

Devils and wolverines have heavy builds, short powerful limbs, small round ears, weak eyesight, an excellent sense of smell and large heads to support their powerful jaws. (A wolverine skull in David Pemberton's office in the Tasmanian Museum and Art Gallery is often mistaken for a devil skull.) Both animals have white neck and throat patches, and are occasional tree climbers—only juveniles in the case of devils, while generally wolverines are 'not considered to display arboreal behaviour'.[7]

Devils and wolverines are habitually described as nocturnal animals, but both species can be active during daylight. They are both regularly described as bear-like, due particularly to the shape of the head, the small eyes and round ears, broad chest when upright, glossy coat and pronounced claws. One of the Wolverine Foundation's Frequently Asked Questions is whether the Tasmanian devil is a biological relative of the wolverine. ('No . . . They may resemble each other physically, however they are distinctly different.')[8]

Adult wolverines typically weigh 2–3 kilograms more than adult devils, much of which is fat for insulation, while their fur is long and thick and their pads broad for travelling in snow. Wolverines have low density distribution; devil densities vary from low to very high. Wolverines have an inbuilt fearlessness and will not hesitate to attack if threatened, whereas devils generally are timid. Wolverines use strong scents to mark their territory, which devils do not conspicuously do, being non-territorial (although devil latrines may serve a similar function). Wolverines, as solitary animals, are quiet, as are solitary devils, though both have a range of social vocalisations.

Like the devil, the wolverine's food habits 'are weighted to scavenging'.[9] Wolverines are unfussy, opportunistic eaters and will cover large amounts of territory in search of food. They are known to attack incapacitated animals much larger than themselves but are generally recognised as voracious scavengers, so much so that early North American settlers nicknamed them Gluttons. Eggs, insects, birds, rodents, squirrels and hares all form part of their diet.

Convergent evolution is strongly evident in the reason for both devils and wolverines having very powerful jaws: the wolverine is a specialist bone-crusher, capable of crunching through an elk or moose femur for the valuable marrow. It also chews frozen meat.

Both have been hunted for their persistent, opportunistic preying on animals trapped for their fur—wallabies and possums in Tasmania, mink and marten in the northern hemisphere. And just as the devil had a bounty placed on it for supposedly killing lambs in Tasmania's early days of white settlement, wolverines continue to be bounty-hunted across Scandinavia for their predation upon domestic reindeer and sheep.

Again, not unlike the devil, the wolverine is often regarded as a nuisance or worse, not least for its powerful, rank chemical secretions. In Native American folklore the wolverine is an ambivalent hero-trickster and a link to the spirit world. Interestingly, in North America it is sometimes called the Indian devil, and a 2002 video produced by the Wolverine Foundation is entitled *Wolverine: Devil of the North?*

The ratel, despite its common name of honey badger, is no longer classed in the badger sub-family. True badgers tend to be omnivores; ratels are predator–scavengers with a much greater tendency to carnivory. Hence, 'In 1902 it was transferred to the Mustelidae on the basis of skull morphology and teeth [and] in 1912 a kinship with the wolverine *Gulo gulo* was suggested.'[10]

Ratels occur throughout Africa—parts of the Sahara excepted—the Middle East and India. Not surprisingly, given that vast distribution, they are adapted to many forms of habitat, from dense wet rainforest to semi-arid desert and sub-alpine

The ratel, like the devil, is both a predator and scavenger. They have very powerful jaws. (Courtesy Mike Myers, Wilderness Safaris)

heights. Devils showed a similar widespread distribution across the Australian mainland, and they occupy all parts of Tasmania.

The ratel's lower body is black, the upper body light, although colouration varies according to habitat; they are paler in more arid regions. It is not inconceivable that mainland desert devils may have displayed some degree of colour adaptation.

Devils and ratels are thickset and low to the ground; ratels weigh slightly more than devils and have a proportionately longer body. The ratel has 'a massive head with a thick skull'.[11] The jaw is powerful, though unlike the devil's this may not be just for hunting and eating but also for defence: although considered 'shy and retiring',[12] it has a well-known propensity for aggression against animals much larger than itself.

The devil's peculiar lope is one of its most distinctive features, matched, however, by that of the ratel, which has a 'slow, rather bow-legged lumbering gait that sometimes increases to a clumsy gallop'.[13] Yet both, the ratel especially, are capable of running at considerable speed.

Convergent evolution is particularly evident in the diets of these unrelated, small, tough, nocturnal nomads. Devils eat 'everything'—from tadpoles to dead cows and horses—and one of the first surveys of ratels in the wild, undertaken in the late 1990s in the Kalahari Desert by zoologists Keith and Colleen Bigg, found likewise; ratels 'proved to be great opportunists, eating a range of 61 different species . . . food as small as social and solitary bee larvae, geckoes, scorpions, rodents and snakes to larger prey including springhares . . . birds and the juveniles of jackals . . . wildcat . . . fox'.[14]

Devils are closest of all to hyaenas, in particular the brown hyaena, which tends towards nocturnalism and solitariness, whereas spotted and striped hyaenas live in social clans of up to 80 with a rigid female-dominated hierarchy. Hyaenas and devils have a number of similarities: a shuffling lope resulting from a powerful forebody (hyaenas' rear legs are actually shorter than the forelegs); an ability to consume up to a third of their body weight at one feed, whether carrion or fresh kill; like the devil, brown hyaenas regularly forage on beaches (their range takes in the Western Cape, Namibia and Angola); hyaenas use communal latrines for social purposes; the vocalisations of hyaenas—screams, giggles, whoops, growls and snarls—match or exceed the devil's in range and complexity.

Hyaenas have a large sagittal crest on top of the skull for muscle attachment, giving the jaws great power—they are able to work their way through large bones. A frequently asked question is: Which species has the most powerful jaw: the hyaena, the wolverine or the Tasmanian devil? Some studies

Covergent evolution is evident in the range of similarities between the brown hyaena and the Tasmanian devil, including a tendency towards nocturnalism and solitariness. (Courtesy Mike Myers, Wilderness Safaris)

credit the Bengal tiger, the estuarine crocodile and the devil with the greatest jaw strength, though pound-for-pound rodents are probably way ahead—but they in turn must give way to ants!

Ignorance and superstition branded the hyaena a cowardly scavenger. Among its supposedly demonic attributes was an ability to change sex at will. The reality is that male and female hyaena genitalia are very similar, because females have a high testosterone count. Eric Guiler, intriguingly, claimed to have witnessed consecutive hermaphroditism—sex reversal—in a number of captured devils. David Pemberton and Nick Mooney, trapping devils at Granville Harbour in 2004, observed a devil with a non-functional pouch and scrotum.

One of the hyaena's practical functions, disposing of human corpses, may well have led many Africans to regard it with unease. There are still some remote tribes of Maasai and Karama-jong, however, for whom this method of corpse disposal is delivery of the individual's spirit to the afterlife. It has an interesting echo of the wolverine's link to the spirit world in Native American mythology. In pre-European Tasmania, might the devil have had such a relationship with the indigenous humans?

In a role not dissimilar to that historically attributed to devils—that they followed thylacines and ate the remains of their prey—hyaenas were incorrectly portrayed as bickering scavengers cleaning up after lion kills. Although scavenging is important, all three species of hyaena are active, highly successful pursuit predators. And like devils, they will opportunistically eat their own.

Despite the relationship between the Tasmanian devil and the thylacine, the devil is taxonomically closer to the other members of the Dasyuridae family, the quolls and the tiny mice-like marsupials—dibblers, antechinuses, kowaris, mulgaras, kalutas, phascogales, planigales, ningauis, dunnarts and kultarrs. (The more distantly related numbats, bandicoots, bilbies and the marsupial mole make up the rest of Australia's sub-order of carnivorous marsupials.)

Quolls are well covered with spotted fur, have long tails, pointed facial features and sharp teeth. Two of the four species are found in Tasmania, the abundant eastern quoll (*Dasyurus vivevrinus*, once called the native cat) and the larger, less common spotted-tailed quoll (*D. maculatus*, tiger cat), which weighs up to 7 kilograms. Both species were once common across the mainland, but the eastern quoll is extinct there now and its larger cousin reduced to rump populations. Quolls are excellent hunters and prey on many invertebrates, reptiles, rodents, possums and small macropods. They climb very well, and birds and sugar gliders are included in their prey. But carrion also forms an important part of the diet, while rubbish-dump scavenging, poultry raiding, corbey grubs and fruit all add to an impressively varied diet.

The great mammalogist John Eisenberg visited Tasmania in 1990 on sabbatical. He had recently published *The Mammalian Radiations*, the most comprehensive summary of mammal evolution to date. Earlier in his career he had published studies of the behaviour of Tasmanian devils, and while in Tasmania he discussed with zoologists the concept of the carnivore guild and its functioning as a unit. His seminal thoughts and discussions contributed to the work and management directions which followed.

In his book (subtitled *An Analysis of Trends in Evolution, Adaptation and Behaviour*) Eisenberg first conceptualised the importance of studying a marsupial carnivore guild rather than individuals in isolation.[15] Menna Jones' resulting guild-structure findings derive from dentition studies carried out in the field and on skulls held in Australian collections. She showed that the relationship between devils and quolls evolved as one of direct competition. She sought to determine the role of such competition in structuring body size, habitat usage and diet. In general, species will space out in a habitat according to their own size and the size of their prey. It is called equal spacing.

A major finding was that, for this to be achieved, 'the spotted-tailed quoll had to redefine itself in an evolutionary sense'.[16] And it happened quickly: Jones puts the evolutionary timescale of this at as little as 100 to 200 generations, a generation being two years. While devils and the small eastern quoll are sufficiently different in size as to have minimal dietary overlap, the larger spotted-tailed quoll is in the middle, and

The spotted-tailed quoll competes with the devil for both live prey and carrion. Devils are frequently blamed for raiding poultry yards, when quolls are the more likely culprit. The spotted-tailed quoll, once commonly known as the tiger cat, is extinct across most of mainland Australia and no longer common in Tasmania. (Courtesy Dave Watts)

therefore in competition with both. Jones believes that this may explain why it is the rarest of the three. How did she arrive at these conclusions?

Skulls and skeletal material held in collections across Australia were measured. Particular attention was paid to dentition, with arrays of data compiled to create an index of tooth strength, as opposed to mere changes in tooth size over time. As well, the size and therefore strength of the *temporalis* muscles, the jaw-closing muscles, were measured by dimensions taken off the skulls. Tooth strength and jaw strength determine the size of prey a particular species can take. Analysis of the data indicated 'intense competition in Tasmania . . . anything other than equal spacing means two species are going to rub up against each

This photograph offers rare proof of the predatory ability of the spotted-tailed quoll. This one has chased down and is killing a pademelon. (Courtesy Michael Good)

other, hence enforced equal spacing. We got equal spacing in the jaw-closing muscle, tooth strength, and average prey size. That's pretty neat.'[17] Estimates are that the eastern quoll is three times as abundant and the (pre-disease) devil six times as abundant as the spotted-tailed quoll.

As the Australian continent dried out and heated up, the paucity of grazing or browsing vegetation shrank not only the megafauna but their replacements as well. Yet in this respect the Tasmanian devil is a veritable giant. Quolls aside, an adult male devil is up to 150 times larger than its closest marsupial relatives. They're also completely unalike, an indication of how varied the evolution of Australia's marsupial carnivores has been.

Thus the swamp antechinus (*Antechinus minimus*, 'smallest hedgehog equivalent') distributed across Tasmania and coastal Victoria, weighs about 65 grams. A strictly nocturnal insect

A male dusky antechinus in its favourite habitat of forest leaf litter. The tiny antechinus, weighing just 65 grams, is closely related to the Tasmanian devil. Males die within three weeks of mating, a feature of young devils since the onset of DFTD. (Courtesy W.E. Brown)

eater and ground dweller—unlike the even smaller brown antechinus (*A. stuartii*) which likes to live in trees—this tiny marsupial is described as the smallest of the quolls. A unique feature of the antechinuses is semelparousness, the death of the male after sex. (It is also a feature of the life cycles of squid and flying ants.)

The little red antechinus (*Antechinus rosamondae*), which weighs about 40 grams and preys vigorously on lizards, seems to owe its precarious existence along the mid-north coast of Western Australia to the fire-resistant, inedible woolly spinifex in which it lives.

The kowari (*Dasyuroides byrnei*) of central Australia, one of a number of marsupial species that become torpid during cold weather, is also a fierce hunter and vocally aggressive:

A variety of sounds are produced, including an open-mouthed hissing and a loud, staccato chattering, both made in response to threats from predators or other kowaris . . . Vigorous tail-switching, reminiscent of an angry cat, is used as a threat display.[18]

The red-tailed phascogale (*Phascogale calura*) survives in Australia's arid centre through an impressive adaptation: it is immune to the poisonous plants upon which it feeds, as are the native carnivores which prey upon it. But the poison fluoro-acetate, found in the Australian legumes *Gastrolobium* spp. and *Oxylobium* spp., kills introduced species.

An unusual adaptation is that of the long-tailed planigale (*Planigale ingrami*), one of the world's smallest mammals (the average male adult weighs 4.2 grams). Its head is flattened so that it can enter cracks and narrow spaces in search of the insects, lizards and small mammals which it attacks with ferocity.

A species as endangered as the spotted-tailed quoll, and matching the devil for size, now has full claim on being Tasmania's top order predator. The wedge-tailed eagle is a supreme hunter, one of the world's largest eagles. This majestic raptor, although distributed across Australia and New Guinea, is listed as vulnerable in Tasmania (subspecies *Aquila audax fleayi*). Its diet is a practical one, relying generally on possums, wallabies, rabbits, hares, birds and carrion. This means that wedge-tailed eagles and devils are direct competitors.

The eagle, like the thylacine, has long been demonised as a lamb-killer and has endured heavy persecution. Indeed, the formation in 1884 of the Buckland and Spring Bay Tiger and Eagle Extermination Society set in motion the Tasmanian parlia-mentary debates that were to signal the extermination of the

The wedge-tailed eagle, one of the world's largest birds of prey, is considered to be Tasmania's top order predator now that the thylacine is extinct. Human alteration to the land, as well as direct persecution, have adversely affected both species for over two hundred years. The parent bird is on the right. (Courtesy W.E. Brown)

If the European red fox becomes established in Tasmania, as it is on mainland Australia as an introduced species, it will compete directly with the devil—for prey, for dens and as a predator of devil young. In combination with DFTD, the fox may unwittingly hasten the Tasmanian devil's extinction. (Courtesy W.E. Brown)

thylacine. Well over a century later the 'wedgie' continues to be persecuted, with some rural Tasmanians taking a gun to it when they can.

Finally, there is the European red fox, long established on the mainland as an introduced species and potentially becoming established in Tasmania. Just as the devil may have inadvertently hastened the end of the thylacine, an ineradicable fox population may do the same to a heavily decreased devil population. But should this eventuate, the highly competitive, efficient fox should not be made the scapegoat for having been introduced to Tasmania.

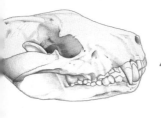

4 'MADE FOR TRAVELLING ROUGH': DEVIL ECOLOGY

Little Devil only wanted milk for several days given by a bottle while being cradled in my arms and loved being cuddled and would emit the most piercing sound when he had finished feeding. Little Devil lived in an old meat safe near the pot belly stove during the day in the kitchen and at night would come out for his meat and biscuits, but should anyone other than myself be in the kitchen he would retreat until all was quiet . . . Eventually the kitchen door was left ajar so he could come in and out at night, this happened for some time before he decided he was old enough to make it on his own. I guess like all teenagers he grew up. It will always remain one of my most treasured memories.

DONNA COLEMAN, GORDON

In its evolutionary journey the Tasmanian devil has travelled remarkably well. And quickly: known devil fossils date back no more than 70 000 years and over that time the animal has undergone little change to its body plan other than dwarfism. Its physical and behavioural characteristics helped ensure its success as one of the seven extant large-size marsupial carnivores of Australia and New Guinea.

The squat, muscular body and short strong legs enable it to lope long hours in search of food and, in the case of males, reproductive partners. Because they are large, the head and neck have increased functional significance in feeding. The devil's profuse, wiry vibrissae (whiskers) grow in patches from the tip of the chin to the back of the jawline, and are long enough to extend beyond shoulder width, acting as sensors during night movement, feeding and communication.

Devils, like dogs, have 42 teeth. (Cats have just 30.) Devils keep their original teeth, which continue to grow very slowly throughout the lifetime of the animals—they are not replaced.

The long claws are designed to dig efficiently, for denning and in search of food, and to firmly grip prey to facilitate chewing and gnawing. The sense of smell is acute and can detect food up to a kilometre away.

This structural emphasis on feeding places the devil in the company of one of nature's iconic loners, the great white shark. A big old male devil has a shark-like forward torso, resulting in a great neck and head with a full but definite taper, providing immense power, out of proportion to the overall body.

The reproductive cycle of the devil is highly synchronised, but not inflexible. Female devils ovulate up to three times during the three-week breeding season, usually in late March, and copulation is almost continuous for up to five days at a time. The male goes to great lengths to keep other males away from his mating partner, keeping her prisoner in the copulation den with little chance to eat or drink. One thirsty male was observed dragging a female with him from a den to a water source and back to the den.[1] David Pemberton and the Mount William ranger Steve Cronin once monitored a male and female in an underground mating den in the wild. The animals hadn't moved from it for eight days and nights, so, wondering if they had died, Pemberton dug a narrow hole through to the burrow and put his arm down, holding a small mirror. His colleague shone a torch onto the mirror, which revealed a threatening set of bared devil teeth.

However, the intensity of male competition generally ensures that during a normal breeding season males breed with more than one female. Menna Jones' studies of breeding indicate that females can be selective, and this means that in combination with multiple sperm donors the female optimises her chances of delivering the best available genetic offspring.

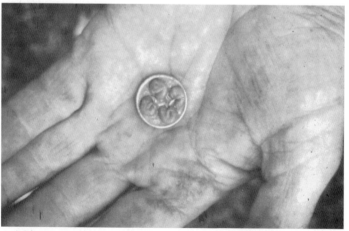

At birth, Tasmanian devils are tiny, as shown by these four newborns on a coin.
(Courtesy Nick Mooney)

At birth a Tasmanian devil is no larger or heavier than a split pea. A prime four-year-old male is some 15 000 times heavier, at about 11 kilograms. (In comparison, from birth to maturity the average domestic cat increases in weight about 20-fold.) At six years the male will be dead, having sired perhaps sixteen offspring. An adult female, weighing about 7 kilograms, has on average four breeding seasons, producing about twelve offspring during her lifetime. The mating season is three weeks; pregnancy lasts just eighteen days; the young are dependent on their mother for at least nine months, which means the female then has little time to herself before the next mating season. This demanding cycle means devil populations can theoretically double in size each year, an excellent safeguard against high mortality in both juvenile and adult populations.

A female devil has four nipples in her marsupium and litters of three or four pups are common, which helps balance out the high juvenile mortality rate. David Pemberton found a healthy 80 per cent of two-year-olds carrying pouch young during his fieldwork study. The mother stands to give birth. Twenty or more tiny embryos leave the womb and travel up to the backward-opening pouch in a stream of mucus. The first arrivals clamp to the teats, which swell in their mouths, so that the newborns become firmly attached to their mother. This ensures they do not fall out of the pouch and is an important survival factor.

Devils are usually born in mid-April, that is, mid-autumn, ensuring they won't be weaned and have to face the world alone until long after Tasmania's challenging winter has passed. DFTD, however, has produced a dramatic shift in reproductive behaviour, with a scatter of births across the seasons rather than

Baby devils begin to grow fur when they are twelve weeks old. Their sturdy tail is as long as their torso and has important functions including balance, storage of fat and communication. (Courtesy Collection Tasmanian Museum and Art Gallery)

exclusively in autumn, and a high number of males competing for perhaps just one receptive female.

In 1934 David Fleay managed to breed devils in captivity and wrote a fine, precise account of it:

In the first days of June four tiny, pink, naked and blind babies each a half inch in length had betaken themselves to their mother's pouch. Shortly after this the father was removed to bachelor quarters, for the mother now showed resentment at his presence by whining growls which rose abruptly in pitch and volume whenever the male attempted to enter the rock shelter. Early in August at the age of seven weeks the thick-set babies in the pouch had grown to a length of two and three quarter inches. They were still pink and hairless but now it could be seen that their tiny limbs moved actively as they clung tenaciously to the teats within the pouch. They also made slight squeaking noises and with increasing bulk the hind quarters of one quadruplet projected from the pouch as the mother moved about.

Meanwhile she had become somewhat fastidious for a Devil, disdaining raw meat but delighting in rats, birds, eggs, frogs and rabbit heads. Towards the middle of August a great change came over the appearance of the youngsters as the ear tips and then other regions of the skin began to show dark pigment. The pouch too, developing with the family, was far more relaxed and roomy. At eleven weeks the dark pigment of the young had become sufficiently pronounced to throw into strong contrast the future white chest and rump markings. The quiet nervous mother accepted the frequent handling with no sign of resentment. Progress of the little Devils was now quite phenomenal and on October 1st at fifteen weeks of age they first released their till then continuous grip on the teats. They were well furred and their eyes had opened. From these observations it is obvious that the mother must carry her cumbersome family with her for at least fifteen weeks after their birth. But from this time on the youngsters may be left at home in the nest, allowing the mother the freedom necessary for successful 'scrounging'.

When lifted away from the parent the youngsters uttered anxious yapping cries and on being released again clung quickly to the fur of her sides with teeth and fingers—the fore-paws having unusual grasping powers so that the young Devils are expert climbers. On being disturbed from sleep when sheltered by the mother's body, the little fellows lost no time in gripping her extended teats, from which it was almost impossible to dislodge them until firm pressure with a finger-tip over the nostrils caused their mouths to open. At the age of eighteen weeks the 'play age' was apparent . . . At twenty weeks they were seven and three quarter inches in body length with small tails adding a further three inches. They still clung tenaciously to the mother's teats when drinking . . . It was five months before they ceased to rely on their mother's milk for nourishment and unfortunately we lost two of them before they had abandoned the maternal apron strings. One squeezed through the chain netting of the enclosure and was never heard of again while the other sickened and died. The mother and remaining two youngsters showed the thorough scavenging traits of their kind by immediately devouring the whole carcass, except the head, of their deceased relative even though food was plentiful.[2]

Devils are weaned in summer, between December and February, after which they disperse widely, but with a higher proportion of females remaining in the natal areas. Up to 60 per cent die before reaching maturity, according to Guiler. Even so, the sudden increase in numbers over summer can give the appearance of a plague, because juveniles are more crepuscularly active than adults and at dusk are regularly seen on roads, scavenging in paddocks or on beaches and around farm complexes.

Newly weaned devils become solitary at once. They are agile foragers, taking a wide variety of small invertebrates and vertebrates, and their excellent climbing ability enables them to obtain food from trees, such as grubs, and eggs from birds' nests. They are fully grown and mature by the age of two.

The uniqueness of a solitary animal surviving through communal feeding sets the devil apart from other carnivores. Young devils quickly learn to congregate at the site of a carcass, drawn by the scent and, just as importantly, the vocalisations of

Young devils are agile foragers and good climbers. This picture was taken at Mrs Roberts' Beaumaris Zoo in the early 1900s. (Courtesy Collection Tasmanian Museum and Art Gallery)

those that have already arrived at the site. Conflict over a carcass is avoided through a ritualised behaviour ensemble.

Young devils, because they are active at dusk, have the advantage of arriving at food sources before the more competitive adults. This, however, puts them into competition with spotted-tailed quolls, which are also active diurnal feeders.

Feeding devils communicate with each other through a range of visual postures, vocalisations and a suite of chemical signals. It was once assumed that dasyurids made little use of visual communications because they are nocturnal. Devils have night-adapted eyesight and their white chest and rump flashes are distinctly visible at night. Interaction between devils at feeding sites takes the form of a ritualised contest, with the dominant feeder not being displaced until it has gorged itself.

A devil eats up to 40 per cent of its body weight per meal every two to three days. Eating such a large quantity of food in a short space of time—about half an hour on average—often results in the animal waddling off with a distended belly and lying down not far from the feeding site; a devil in this state is easy to approach. It is likely that the absence of other large predators has facilitated this form of feeding, even during the long period when thylacines were Australia's largest carnivore. This lends some support to the belief that thylacines ate only choice parts of their prey, leaving the rest to devils and other scavengers.

Being a scavenger able to digest a wide variety of food matter—flesh, fish, bone, invertebrates, fruit, vegetation—was an advantage to the devil's survival. It may also be that the thylacine's narrower food base (and less productive breeding cycle) meant that it existed in comparatively lower numbers, leaving it more vulnerable to changed circumstances (human predation) than the devil.

The number of devils feeding together is generally determined by the size of a carcass: groups of two to five are common. The first arrival is the dominant feeder (unlike communal hyaena feeding, where the higher ranking clan members feed before subordinates), which makes way for a challenger once it has gorged itself. The size of the carcass affects the extent to which the feeding devil will chase off a challenger: the feeder defends the amount of food it needs, not the entire carcass.

Satiation, rather than dominance, is the most likely information conveyed by the ritualised interactions. This means all devils, small and large, resident and transient, can feed together. It is an efficient way of sustaining a population.

David Pemberton was the first to make scientific field studies of devils feeding in the wild. The absence of unrestrained aggression while feeding, and the complex behaviour occurring in its place, was a critical discovery, overturning popular (and some professional) perceptions of the animal, as in this supposedly informed 1984 account of feeding devils by a popular natural history author: 'They behave like a brawling mob, having, so far as anyone knows, virtually no social organisation or restraining instincts'.[3]

Pemberton recorded only one instance of physical injury in 119 interactions during feeding, with one animal chasing and biting another on the rump. On two occasions he also observed jaw-wrestling, where devils stood on their hind legs with forepaws on each other's shoulders or chest and their jaws interlocked. The animals vocalised constantly while shaking their heads from side to side. Although there was no obvious physical damage to the animals, the nature of the interaction appeared as if it could have caused extensive damage to muzzles or jaws. On each occasion the defeated animal ran off into the bush with its tail in the air and fur fully erect, with the winner pursuing it and biting its rump whenever it was close enough.[4]

Examination of 150 trapped animals showed that 6 per cent had suffered injuries consistent with fighting during feeding or breeding, showing enough damage to the flesh of the face to leave teeth visible. These, however, were aged males with lame hindquarters and extensive hair loss on rump and tail, suggesting a physical deterioration other than that caused by intra-specific aggression. A third showed some form of wound, such as puncture holes on the back and rump and shortened, hairless tails. It doesn't automatically mean that all the wounds were obtained while feeding; in fact, most wounds occur during the breeding season.

Pemberton recorded eight vocalisations between initiators and recipients at carcasses: a 'snort' made by expelling air through nostrils and mouth; a short, deep, low-intensity 'humf growl', often repeated; a short, deep, high-energy 'bark', seldom repeated; a 'clap' made by snapping the jaws together; mono-tone, vibrato or crescendo 'growl-whines'; a 'screech', associated with defeat; a 'sneeze' and a 'yip'.[5]

Pemberton also identified some 20 postures that reinforce the elaborate nature of the feeding interactions. They include:

- Neck threat—one nips at the neck area of the other, without making contact. These nips are repeated and the recipient responds by shouldering the initiator or attacking it face on.
- Gape—animals open their jaws for a few seconds as inter-actions take place.
- Lying down—the initiator of the behaviour lies down on its belly with the fore and hind feet extended. These animals are in full view of the possessor of the carcass, but do not physi-cally interact with it.
- Sitting—the initiator sits and stares in the direction of the recipient, often combining this with gaping and lying down.
- Head and tail positions—these vary from a frequent 'head-up-tail-down' posture to a less frequent 'head-up-tail-straight' posture. Their intensity seems to be reflected by

Devils regularly use communal latrines, as this area of scats clearly shows. The latrines are believed to function like community noticeboards. (Courtesy Nick Mooney)

the degree to which the fur on the tail is raised. In some circumstances the legs are bent sufficiently for the belly to scrape on the ground.

- Tripod—the initiator raises one front paw off the ground while facing another animal, with the head held up and the tail down.
- Stiff legged—the initiator moves forward a short distance without flexing the joints of the legs.
- Urinating—the initiator urinates in full view of the recipient, sometimes in conjunction with stiff legs or gape. This action may also facilitate a chemical signal to the recipient.
- Ano-genital drag—the animal presses its anus and genitals against the ground and drags itself along with its forepaws, while holding its chest off the ground. This posture is sometimes accompanied by gaping and an erect tail. It may also be

associated with the transmission of chemical signals. Characteristic drag lines are often seen at communal latrine sites (and are easily mistaken for wallaby tail marks).

Devil literature sometimes refers to ano-genital dragging as cloacal dragging, but this term is inaccurate. Males as well as females engage in dragging, and they begin doing so well before being weaned. Although scent marking is associated with territoriality in many animal species, the function of dragging is not fully known.

Dens and home ranges are key aspects to understanding devil behaviour in the wild. Devils regularly use three or four dens, preferring wombat burrows, dense vegetation near creeks, thick grass tussocks, and caves where they are available. Old wombat burrows and caves are favoured maternity dens, no doubt because of their relative security from predators. Once established in dens adults tend to use them for life.

Devil pups cling to their mother when she needs to transport them. (David Fleay)

While adult devils alternate between dens, dependent denned young are not generally moved from one to another. Thus, while mothers with young have a fixed location, all other devils move around. It is apparent from this that the locality of dens forms an integral aspect of the spatial organisation of devils, as well as being critical to survival of the young. In this way the devil is more dependent on its den than its larder. The same applies to the wolverine, which also dens its young in a fixed locality. Studies have shown that habitat disruption, while it may not negatively affect the local food supply, exposes these natal dens and increases mortality as a result. When this occurs, the mother moves with the young clinging to her back; this greatly increases their vulnerability.

Habitat interference affects animals by altering the refuges where they breed, raise young and rest. For the devil this could be critical. Maternity dens are carefully selected to provide a safe haven from the elements and from scavengers. Young devils get cold easily and need the warmth of their nests and the sun. Favoured dens are strongly protected and may have existed for centuries. Destroying them through, for example, land clearance, disrupts population stability. Reduction in suitable denning habitat has significantly affected the wolverine.

The location and shape of home ranges appear to be controlled by the distribution of food, primarily wallabies and pademelons, both of which are present in large numbers in many parts of Tasmania. Both male and female adult devils are active between sunset and sunrise, travelling up to 16 kilometres a night in search of food. In this way they cover the extent of the home range, generally in a circular pattern. Males and females have similar sized home ranges, which is unusual in sexually dimorphic, solitary carnivores. Larger males obtain the additional food they need by eating for longer. While engaged on his doctoral research David Pemberton charted one devil's home range, which 'took in three hectares of the Musselroe Bay holiday village and tip site'.[6]

In the 10 000 years in which they have lived isolated in Tasmania, the devil's predator competitors—thylacine, wedge-tailed eagle, spotted-tailed quoll—have not threatened the survival of the species. Furthermore, apart from during the mating season and occasionally while feeding, devils do not engage in combat with one another. This is why, even though solitary, they are able to live together in high densities and share overlapping home ranges. Thirty devils weighing a combined 250 kilograms equates to many fewer bears or hyaenas occupying the same space. Even so, consider a Tasmanian farmer's anxiety if he had six hyaenas living in his back paddocks.

5 DEVILS AND EUROPEANS, 1803–1933

The devil stories I was told as a farm boy were shot through with menace. Devils were as dangerous as the name suggested. In large packs they stalked and harassed pregnant, sick or dying cows and horses. If the stricken animal refused to fall the pack leaders would bite clean through its front legs and the rest would swoop in . . . I can see now that the old men and women who said they knew for a fact that devils attacked animals many times their size were just trying to protect me from the dangers of the bush. But they were also voicing the fears they had inherited from those early convicts who were being literal when they named the carnivores they had newly encountered after the Prince of Darkness.

RODNEY CROOME, HOBART

In 1803 an attempt to establish a convict colony at Port Phillip Bay (subsequently Melbourne) proved unsuccessful and led instead to the settlement of the penal colony of Van Diemen's Land. A member of the small founding group was George

Prideaux Harris who, in Hobart Town, worked as a lawyer, journalist, surveyor and natural historian. He became the first European to describe and classify the devil, naming the squat, peculiar little animal *Didelphis ursina*. The name he gave the genus echoes the American opossum, while the species name was intended to reflect its bearlike (ursine) qualities, not least the small round ears. Harris correctly noted a number of similarities between the devil and the thylacine, one being a marsupial trademark, that the rear heels of both are long and callous.

George Prideaux Harris, after whom the devil is named, wrote the first description of the animal in 1806:

> These animals were very common on our first settling at Hobart Town, and were particularly destructive to poultry, &c. They, however, furnished the convicts with a fresh meal, and the taste was said to be not unlike veal. As the settlement increased, and the ground became cleared, they were driven from their haunts near the town to the deeper recesses of forests yet explored. They are, however, easily procured by setting a trap in the most unfrequented parts of the woods, baited with raw flesh, all kinds of which they eat indiscriminately and voraciously; they also, it is probable, prey on dead fish, blubber, &c. as their tracks are frequently found on the sands of the sea shore.
>
> In a state of confinement, they appear to be untameably [sic] savage; biting severely, and uttering at the same time a low yelling growl. A male and female, which I kept for a couple of months chained together in an empty cask, were continually fighting; their quarrels began as soon as it was dark (as they slept all day), and continued throughout the night almost without intermission, accompanied with a kind of hollow barking, not unlike a dog, and sometimes a sudden

George Prideaux Harris, the deputy Surveyor General in the first party of Britons to settle Van Diemen's Land, drew these devil and thylacine sketches for the Linnean Society of London in 1806. (Courtesy Linnean Society of London)

kind of snorting, as if the breath was retained a considerable time, and then suddenly expelled. The female generally conquered. They frequently sat on their hind parts, and used their fore paws to convey food to their mouths. The muscles of their jaws were very strong, as they cracked the largest bones with ease asunder; and many of their actions, as well as their gait, strikingly resembled those of the bear . . . Its vulgar name is the Native Devil.[1]

Fifty years after Harris wrote his description of the devil, the English naturalist and artist John Gould compiled his three-volume *Mammals of Australia* and his seven-volume *Birds of Australia*, both brilliant and enduring records. Gould, who predicted the thylacine's demise nearly a century before its extinction, wrote of the Tasmanian devil:

> [I]ts black colouring and unsightly appearance obtained for it
> the trivial names of Devil and Native Devil. It has now become
> so scarce in all the cultivated districts, that it is rarely if ever,
> seen there in a state of nature; there are yet, however, large
> districts in Van Diemen's Land untrodden by man; and such

Famous naturalist John Gould described many species of Australian fauna in the mid-nineteenth century and had an array of artists working for him, including Henry Richter who drew this devil from a live specimen in London's Zoological Society menagerie. Unusually for a Gould work of art, it's anatomically incorrect, having a small, underslung jaw. (Courtesy David Owen)

localities, particularly the rocky gullies and vast forests on the western side of the island, afford it a secure retreat. During my visit to the continent of Australia I met with no evidence that the animal is to be found in any of its colonies, consequently Tasmania alone must be regarded as its native habitat.

In its disposition it is untameable and savage in the extreme, and is not only destructive to the smaller kangaroos and other native quadrupeds, but assails the sheep-folds and hen-roosts whenever an opportunity occurs for its entering upon its destructive errand.

Although the animal has been well known for so many years, little or nothing more has been recorded respecting it than that which appeared in the ninth volume of the Linnean Society's Transaction from the pen of Mr Harris . . .[2]

Writing in 1880, author and artist Louisa Anne Meredith did much to publicise the new British colony. Her books were very popular in England and her chatty, hotchpotch style says as much about Victorian readers as it does the animal under scrutiny:

[I]f anyone desires to see a blacker, uglier, more savage, and more untameable beast than our 'Devil', he must be difficult to please—that's my opinion. I suppose those who bestowed such a name on him had pretty good reasons for it, and knew that they only gave the devil his due . . . I've heard people say in joke, of others who had very wide mouths, that, when they gaped, their heads were off; but it seems true of this animal, his jaws open to such an extent, and a murderous set of fangs they show when they do open!

The head, which is flat, broad, very ugly, and with little skull-room for brains, takes up one-third the whole length of the beast, which is usually from a foot and a-half to two feet, some being larger. The tail sticks stiffly out, as if made of wood, the feet are something like a dog's, only more sprawly, and with very big claws. It is an awkward beast, and cannot go much of a pace at the fastest. On fairish ground, a man can easily run one down.

One day I was out with Papa in the back-run, and we found a devil. I started full tilt after him, and came two or three good croppers amongst the rocks to begin with, but I held on, till all of a sudden he stopped short—I couldn't, so I jumped right over him. He gave a vicious snap at my legs with his big jaws, but, luckily for me, he was a second too late. I turned and knocked him over, and papa came up and finished him— finished killing him, I mean. We don't show the brutes any mercy; they do too much mischief. The young lambs stand no chance at all with them. So we hunt them down, or set traps, or dig pitfalls—any and every way we can destroy them we do. Why, one winter, some years ago, one of Papa's shepherds caught nearly one hundred and fifty! They seem to go about in families or parties; for when you catch one, you are tolerably certain of getting six or seven more, one after another, and then perhaps you will not hear of any for a good while. Of course they are much scarcer than formerly, and a very lucky thing, too.

I don't think I mentioned the fur—but it is not fur, it's longish, very coarse, black hair, almost like horse-hair; and then as to fleas, *they swarm!* One of the men brought a dead one to the house one day for Mamma, and it was laid in the garden. Mamma and Lina were soon down on their knees beside it, peeping at its eyes and teeth and ears and all the rest of it; when Lina said, 'Oh, look; how very curious! There are small, brown scales, like a coat of mail, all over it, under the hair'. Mamma looked where Lina had parted the long hair, and *didn't* she jump! Lina's coat of mail was just a coat of fleas. The *post-mortem* examination was cut very short, I assure you, the 'subject' summarily disposed of, and two or three buckets of water poured on the place where it had lain. A pleasant kind of thing for a pet!

There are two sorts of devils—one is all black, the other has a white tail-tip and a white mark like a cross down the throat and between the fore-legs; but one is just as hideous as the other. I believe you cannot tame them, and I am very sure I shall never try. People who have made the attempt say they are as stupid as they are ferocious, and never seem to know one person more than another, but growl and bite at all alike.[3]

For all her apparently direct association with devils, many of her descriptions are clearly inaccurate, and it's of interest that the drawing of the animal accompanying Meredith's text is a freehand copy of Gould's original, unattributed and minus the background devils. She—or another—likewise copied the famous Gould lithograph of a thylacine pair, an animal admittedly much harder to locate, let alone sketch.

Louisa Anne Meredith died in 1895. In that year, wealthy Hobart socialite Mary Roberts opened a private zoo at Beaumaris House, close to the town. The contrast between the women is stark. Not only did Mary Roberts like devils, she bred them, and in doing so helped shift its image from diabolical and satanic to merely animal. Roberts achieved international fame for her devotion to animal causes, through activities such as her founding of the Anti-Plumage League. But she also had a highly developed business sense, importing wildlife from all over the world, while exporting whatever Tasmanian fauna she could.

Not unlike George Harris almost a century earlier, in 1915 Mary Roberts wrote about the devil for an academic British audience, this time for the London Zoological Society. It's an important and accurate document, given the lack of written information about the devil then and universal ignorance of it. The article is titled 'The Keeping and Breeding of Tasmanian Devils':

> Until I was asked by Mr. A. S. Le Souëf, Director of the Zoological Gardens, Moore Park, New South Wales, early in 1910 to obtain, if possible, Tasmanian Tigers (*Thylacinus cynocephalus*) and Devils (*Sarcophilus harrisii*) for the London Zoological Society, I had never thought of keeping either of these animals in my collection; in fact, they were quite unknown to me except as museum specimens, although I had frequently visited remote parts of our island. I have vivid recollections, however, of how, when a young girl at boarding-school in the late [eighteen] forties, some of the girls from Bothwell, near the Lake District, used to give graphic and terrifying accounts of the Tasmanian Devils with their double row of teeth. This belief is not yet exploded, as it was impressed upon me lately with the utmost confidence by a country visitor that such was the case; he not only believed, but said 'he had seen'. The teeth have been described to me by a scientist as truncated.
>
> Shortly after hearing from Mr. Le Souëf, by means of advertising, writing, etc. I obtained three for the London Society, and having then become thoroughly interested I determined to keep some myself. Since that time a large number have passed through my hands, and more than once I have been 'a woman possessed of seven devils'.
>
> In April 1911 I received a family (a mother and four young), and again in September of the same year a similar lot arrived. The former were very young, and I had the

Mary Roberts owned and operated Beaumaris Zoo in Hobart between 1895 and her death in 1921. She collected animals and birds from all over the world and also maintained a thriving business exporting Australian fauna. She wrote that Tasmanian devils were her favourite creatures. Her insights into their behaviour were in marked contrast to public perceptions of them as stinking vermin. (Courtesy Collection Tasmanian Museum and Art Gallery)

opportunity of watching their growth almost from their first appearance when partly protruding from the pouch. When sending them, the trapper wrote that 'the mother was so quiet, I need not be afraid to pick her up in my arms'. The little ones hung from her pouch (heads hidden in it), and she lay still and motionless as if afraid of hurting them by moving, and allowed me to stroke her head with my hand. However timid they may be, and undoubtedly they are extremely so, growling and showing their teeth when frightened, they always evince this gentleness and stillness when nursing little ones.

The skin of the young, on arrival, had the appearance of a slate-coloured kid glove, the tail darker towards the tip. The hair could be seen growing black and velvety from the head downwards, the latter being hidden in the pouch for some days, and it was interesting to note the progress of the growth of the hair from day to day. The shoulders were covered while the hindquarters were almost, or quite, bare, although a faint streak of white was discernible where the white markings were to come later on. At this early stage, should the mother get up to move about, which she rarely does in the daytime, the young somehow scramble into the pouch again.

This family went later to the London Society, but the second, which came on the 16th of September, I kept for my own pleasure, with the exception of the mother; as she had lost a foot when being trapped, I thought it best to have her destroyed later on. Unfortunately, when they were about half grown one escaped into the garden, and the next morning her mutilated remains were found—she had fallen a victim to our two fox-terriers. The three survivors have been ever since an unfailing source of interest and amusement to my family, to visitors, and myself. When a bone or piece of meat was thrown to them a tug-of-war was always the result, and sometimes a chase into one door and out of the other of the little cave. At other times, while one has been holding on to a bone held in my hand, I have lifted it completely off the ground, while another would cling on round the waist and try to pull it down.

Many visitors from the Commonwealth have heard such exaggerated accounts of the ferocity and ugliness of the Tasmanian Devil (others, again, have believed it to be a myth), that they sometimes express surprise when they see them so lively, sprightly and excited, running out to my call; they then remark, 'the devil is not so black as he is painted'.

Two of these Devils were latterly kept together as a pair, and for the purposes of this article I will call them Billy and

Tasmanian devils at Beaumaris Zoo, c. 1910. (Courtesy Collection Tasmanian Museum and Art Gallery)

Truganini, after the last two survivors of our lost Tasmanian race.[4] These showed no disposition to breed until April 1913, and my observation of them and of many others that I have had in my keeping is, that the disinclination to take up maternal duties is always on the part of the female. I then noticed suddenly a decided change—that Billy would not allow her to come out of their little den; if she did venture when called to be fed, or at other times, he immediately attacked her and would drag her back by the ear, or any other part, but although otherwise cruel, he would carry food in to her. When I called her, it was pitiable to hear her whining; but it was of no avail, for Billy was a relentless tyrant and kept her in strict seclusion for quite ten or twelve days; then early in May he allowed her to be free once more. From thence onward, although they were sometimes peaceable and affectionate, the balance of power was completely on

Truganini's side; she constantly resented his approach by biting and snarling at him: it seemed as if coming events cast their shadows before, and she instinctively felt that he would do the young some injury. From now her pouch was anxiously scanned day by day, but it was some time before I could be sure that it was gradually enlarging. I had been advised by Dr Hornaday, of the New York Zoological Park, that if ever the Tigers or Devils were likely to have young, to remove the male, and as soon as I was certain, I had Billy taken away and placed with the other member of the family. This made Truganini most unhappy, as he was near enough for her to hear him, besides which, the two males fought; so, being cautioned by my family that perhaps my interference might cause a disaster, I yielded and replaced him, doing so with many misgivings. Matters went on much the same until late in September, when to my delight a tail, and at other times part of a small body, could be seen sticking out of the pouch, more especially when she sat up to wash her face, or rolled upon her back; unlike domestic cats, the devils use both paws for washing, placing them together and thus making a cup-like depression which, when thoroughly licked, is rubbed well over the face. Everything looked very promising on the Sunday before Michaelmas Day, when I noticed Truganini carrying large bunches of straw about in her mouth, evidently seeking for a retired place to make a bed, and we had already placed some fern logs in a corner of their yard. As Billy would follow her about and interfere, I had a box put down with a hole cut in the side that she might hide under; but it was of no use, as where she went he would also go, and a scrimmage was the inevitable result. Early next morning, with many misgivings I left home for ten days, only to find on my return that her pouch was empty and that the young had disappeared, and as no remains whatever had been found, I could only conclude that they had been eaten by Billy.

Thus ended all my hopes and anticipations for 1913. I have not so far related an incident that took place just before the breeding-season. Being hopeful that Truganini might have young in her pouch, and my assistant being as usual very busy, Professor T. T. Flynn, of the Tasmanian University, who is always interested in our marsupials, kindly offered to examine her pouch. As soon as an attempt was made to catch her, Billy grasped the position of affairs and fought to defend her with all his might, even getting behind her in the little cave, putting a paw on each shoulder and holding her tightly, lest she might get into what appeared to him to be the danger zone. By dint of perseverance and a little strategy he was outwitted at last, but our hopes were doomed to disappointment.

Truganini has now passed through another period of retirement, and I am hoping to record shortly a greater measure of success for 1914.

I cannot close this article without a few words in defence of the Tasmanian Devil, as I am sure that it is more or less 'misunderstood', and the article with photograph published in the 'Royal Magazine' for October 1913 under the name of L. R. Brightwell, F. Z. S., is, I consider, greatly exaggerated both as regards their appearance and character, viz., 'They are well named, for they tear everything, even sheep, to pieces if they get the chance'.

On several occasions when one of mine has escaped, the only mischief done has been the destruction of a fowl or a duck or two. It would have been just as easy for a wallaby to have been killed if they had had the inclination, about which our fox-terriers would not have hesitated for a minute if a chance had occurred. When in transit to London last year one escaped, and I have been told by the chief officer of the vessel that 'the passengers were much alarmed as there were children on board, and someone went about with a revolver'. Later I came across the butcher who was in charge at the time, and he appeared to have been rather amused than otherwise, and told me the missing one was discovered at last sleeping under the berth of one of the sailors! I don't wonder, with the reputation that the devils have, that the passengers were alarmed.[5]

Mary Roberts had more luck in 1914 when Truganini gave birth to three babies. Billy was again the father but was now kept away from the maternal enclosure. Roberts compiled diary notes, as with these examples:

29th—All three playing like puppies, biting each other and pulling one another about by the ears . . .

30th—Whole family hanging from the mother as she ran out, and one hardly knows which to admire most, her patience and endurance, or the hardihood of the young in holding on and submitting to so much knocking about. The whole process seems very casual and most remarkable . . . The baby devils had the sense of smell very strongly developed; immediately I approached, their nostrils would begin to work and a vigorous sniffing would go on. They were also expert climbers, and although I had some specially constructed yards made, they would get up the wire-netting and walk along the top rail quite easily; at other times they would climb a pear-tree growing in their enclosure and sit in the branches like cats.[6]

Her article concludes with a section headed 'General Remarks':

I have always found devils rather fond of a bath; quite recently, going down to their yard after an illness and finding only a drinking vessel, I ordered a larger one to be put in, and they showed their pleasure by going in at once, sometimes two at a time. I have occasionally poured water from a can over them, when they would run to and fro under it with much enjoyment.

Their sight in daylight is rather defective; they seem to pick up their food more readily by smelling than by seeing, and I think they can see objects better at a distance.

At the present time I have six running together, my own three and three that I bought when in their mother's pouch. All are tame, frolicsome, and lively. I can go in and have a bit of fun with them, and when I am outside their enclosure they frequently climb the wire-netting to the height of nearly six feet, and get their little black faces close to mine with evident delight. We have tried more than once to get them photographed, but it is impossible to keep them quiet, they are on for a scamper all the time. Recently an adult escaped, and it was discovered by a passing school-boy sitting on a high fence bordering the street, under the shade of some elm-trees, many people passing on the foot-path without observing it. They are, however, always very timid when coming down.

They are fond of the sun, and look well when basking in it, the rays shining through make their ears appear a bright red, fore-feet parallel with the head, hind-quarters quite flat on the ground and turned out at right angles, somewhat as a frog.

My sympathy with my little black 'brothers and sisters' is intense, probably evoked by having suffered much mentally owing to the gross cruelties which have come under my notice, the result of capturing them in traps. Frequently three or four have been sent to me in a crate, only to find later on one with a foot shot off or a broken leg. In a consignment received some time ago, a dead one was found; it bore unmistakable signs of a snare previously, round the neck, one foot was gone (an old injury), and finally a recently smashed leg much swollen, the cause of death. I communicated with the S.P.C.A., and since then have had none from that district.

I have derived much pleasure from studying the habits and disposition of the Tasmanian Devils, and have found that they respond to kindness, and certainly show affection and pleasure when I approach them. I have been led to believe that no case of their breeding in captivity has been recorded, and certainly not in Tasmania.

Others who do not know or understand them may think of them as they like, but I, who love them, and have had considerable experience in keeping most of our marsupials, from the Thylacine down to the Opossum Mouse (*Dromica nana*), will always regard them as first favourites, my little black playmates.[7]

Mary Roberts wasn't a trained scientist. But her Beaumaris Zoo not only popularised native animals until then considered loathsome, dangerous and expendable; it also attracted those few scientists who had begun devoting their energies to understanding and protecting the island's fauna. One was Clive Lord, Director of the Tasmanian Museum, who in 1918 compiled a list of about 50 known descriptions, classifications and drawings of the devil. He expressed concern that native species such as the devil were decreasing in numbers while very little was known about them.

Another was Professor T. T. (Theodore Thomson) Flynn, who occupies an important place in Australian zoology as a pioneering twentieth-century mammalogist. His works on the embryology and early development of native animals are rightly

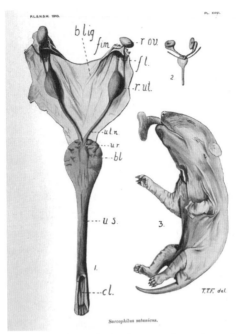

Sarcophilus satanicus.

Professor T.T. (Theodore) Flynn, a biology lecturer and researcher at the University of Tasmania from 1909 to 1930, was the father of actor Errol Flynn. Theodore undertook pioneering laboratory work on devils, one result being this fine natural history illustration of the urogenital system and pup on teat. (Courtesy Collection Tasmanian Museum and Art Gallery)

described as classics. In 1909 he had become the inaugural Professor of Biology at the University of Tasmania and for 20 years remained devoted to his research.

One of Flynn's early publications was 'Contributions to a Knowledge of the Anatomy and Development of the Marsupiala: No. I. The Genitalia of *Sarcophilus satanicus*'. His research derived from a single female devil, the first ever to come into his possession—not from Beaumaris Zoo but from Clive Lord. In his introduction Flynn noted that his intention had been to study a number of specimens before publishing his results, but their 'increased scarcity' decided him otherwise.[8]

The research itself was obviously not easy, Flynn noting the 'unfortunate lack of original communications and papers in Tasmania'.[9] His introductory notes are illuminating:

> The specimen of *Sarcophilus satanicus,* of whose genital organs this communication is a description, was forwarded to me through the kind offices of Mr J. E. C. Lord . . . This is the only female which I have as yet obtained and I had originally intended that its description should wait until further specimens had come to hand; the increased scarcity, however, of these animals, together with the discovery of a number of interesting and significant points in the morphology of the genital organs, has influenced me to publish the results earlier than otherwise would have been the case. Portions of the paper can as yet be regarded only as preliminary notes. This is due, in the first place, to scarcity of material, and, in the second, to an unfortunate lack of original communications and papers in Tasmania.

His short, preparatory description further reveals the difficulties of conducting pioneering scientific work under the conditions he experienced:

> The specimen was a full-grown female, with three fairly advanced young in the pouch. All had been dead for two days. The pouch-young were fixed entire in corrosive-sublimate-acetic-solution, the genital organs of the mother in picro-sulphuric solution. In this latter case, on sectioning, it was found that what blood there was in the vessels had hardened so much, that it was only with extreme care and difficulty that

sections could be cut at all. The hopeless gapping of the razor-edge, with consequent damage to the sections, is well indicated in Fig. 10.[10]

Guiler provides an interesting snapshot of Flynn and Roberts:

> Flynn was a very powerful personality and full of drive and energy which led him into many adventures, creditable and otherwise. He was often at the Zoo in his early days in Tasmania but the [Roberts] Diary entries show a declining enthusiasm and in August 1918 Mrs Roberts records that she had sent an account to Prof. Flynn for the devils, adding that she expected to be paid. In October 1918 she records that she rang the University 're the skeletons Flynn has'; he was to ring back the next day but did not do so. Possibly the non-payment for specimens may have been the cause of Mrs Roberts' annoyance with Flynn but it is not surprising that there was a cooling in their friendship, as Mrs Roberts was most fastidious in all her dealings and Flynn most casual and unbusiness-like in his.[11]

Among Flynn's 'adventures' were rumoured clandestine sales of thylacines. His family life was messy, including estrangement from his wife and considerable difficulty in managing his head-strong, wild, sexually charged son Errol, destined to become the dashing star of more than 50 Hollywood movies. The first chapter of Errol Flynn's autobiography is called 'Tasmanian Devil, 1909–1927', and it was his Hollywood studio, Warner Bros., that created the irrepressible *Looney Tunes* cartoon character, Taz the Tasmanian Devil.

Tasmanian Museum director Clive Lord, in his own writings on the devil, observed:

> Its hardy nature both in captivity and in its wild state cause
> one to wonder how it came about that this species became
> extinct on the mainland within comparatively recent times . . .
> In the rougher sections [of Tasmania] this species exists in fair
> numbers and there is every prospect of it remaining an
> inhabitant of such places for years to come.[12]

Lord also sounded what might be called an optimistic warning, one that has still not been resolved 200 years after George Prideaux Harris wrote his description of the devil. Towards the end of his life Lord wrote: 'We, as Australians, have been placed in charge of a wonderful heritage, and it rests with us to respond to the trusteeship which has been granted us.'[13]

Clive Lord died in 1933 and so did official interest in the devil.

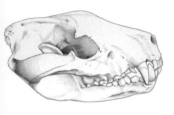

6 IN THE MATTER OF THE SOCIETY AND THE BOARD

A ranger's wife learns to cope with all sorts of emergencies, but the most bizarre was the day I bathed a devil in the laundry tub. He had fallen into the sewerage ponds at Strathgordon. A Hydro worker had watched him swimming frantically around. He was eventually fished out with a pole, exhausted, panting, not looking (or smelling) very good . . . He stayed still, just shivering while I stood him in the warm water and lathered him up, working fast while my luck held. Lifted him out, towelled him down briskly, while he continued to look stunned, then relocated him to the shed, into a wooden box filled with warm blankets, and left him in peace to recover from his ordeal. When the children came home from school we went to the shed, opened the door and the devil bolted to freedom

MAUREEN JOHNSTONE, RIVERSIDE

Throughout the first half of the twentieth century the devil lived in the lengthening shadow thrown by the tiger's disappearance and presumed extinction. But when the devil did receive attention it wasn't good. According to a 1948 tourism publication, devils were 'ugly, bad-tempered and vicious, and settlers have hunted them incessantly with guns and dogs'.[1]

Guiler's pioneering research into devil populations remains of central importance. As a reader in zoology at the University of Tasmania, and chair of the state's Animals and Birds Protection Board in the 1950s and 1960s, he was uniquely placed to study the island's ecology. He provides an interesting potted modern history of the devil:

> This creature did not figure in the debates of the early Boards because, at that time, it was rare to uncommon over all of the State. It was not until 1945 that devils appeared in the Minutes when the Ranger at Lake St Clair was reprimanded for being knowingly involved in the capture of two (or more?) for Poulson's Circus.
>
> By 1950 the numbers had built up to enable the Board to grant permits for their capture and by 1959 pressure was being exerted on the Board to place them on the Unprotected Schedule on account of the damage they did to possums caught by trappers and to weak sheep and lambs. No action was taken other than to grant permits to the complainants provided they could prove the alleged damage.
>
> The depredations became more widespread and by 1966 the Board was issuing poisoning permits to control the devils. However, it was clear that very little was known about devils and a research project was started in 1966 in co-operation with the Zoology Department of the University.
>
> The Board was fortunate in that it had the resources at the time to commence this work as some of the Members were very reluctant to issue poisoning permits for an indigenous species about which so very little was known.

The project was important as it showed that the Board was prepared to switch its resources into non-commercial or non-sporting species and treat them on their scientific merits rather than the political desirability of being seen to be studying the so-called game species. This was the Board's first research programme into a non-game species.[2]

Every year between 1966 and 1975, at remote Granville Harbour on the west coast, Guiler led a devil research team. They set more than 5000 traps at nineteen locations, with such names as Harrison's Back Pockets, Dead Heifer, Duck Creek Track, and Pig Farm. A total of 282 devils was captured 946 times, 664 being recaptures. He also carried out extensive field research at Cape Portland in north-east Tasmania. The published results initiated modern devil research.[3]

Eric Guiler (right) with Eric Reece, a former Premier of Tasmania, at the launch of Guiler's Thylacine: the Tragedy of the Tasmanian Tiger *in 1985. Eric Guiler devoted much of his career to studying thylacines and Tasmanian devils. (Author's collection, Tasmanian Museum and Art Gallery)*

But Guiler didn't have things all his own way. The politics of wildlife conservation and management is as robust in Australia as anywhere else, as he had earlier discovered through the seemingly innocuous and modest trade in zoo animal exports. For six years conservationists repeatedly attacked the Animals and Birds Protection Board for being a key player in the state's fauna export trade.

The saga began in 1957 when the Sydney-based Wild Life Preservation Society of Australia, through its journal *Australian Wild Life*, wrote to the Board expressing concern at the Board's decision to give two Tasmanian devils as a gift to a Swiss zoo. Guiler replied that the director of the Basel Zoological Gardens,

Much of the June 1962 issue of Australian Wild Life: Journal of the Wild Life Preservation Society of Australia *was devoted to the Tasmanian devil and the apparent lack of regard for it by officials of the island state. The New South Wales-based Society's efforts on behalf of the animal may have inspired Tasmania's Animals and Birds Protection Board to commence research into devil populations. (Courtesy Wildlife Preservation Society of Australia Inc.)*

Dr E. M. Lang, had specifically travelled to Hobart to supervise the safe travel of the animals, and that the devil population had increased to such an extent in some parts of the state that 'we have had to make special arrangements to reduce the number owing to their depredations'.[4]

But the Society persisted, querying the legality of the deal and also questioning Lang's proficiency in wildlife management. The journal quoted a report in *The Mercury* in which Lang planned to return to Australia for more exhibits: 'They include the Lyre Bird and Koala Bear, which he is confident can be trained to live on a diet other than gum leaves, which are unprocurable in Europe'.[5]

The fur really began to fly, in the matter of the Society and the Board, with the publication of the June 1962 issue of *Australian Wild Life*. Using a photograph of a demure, attractive juvenile Tasmanian devil on its cover, the journal ran a lengthy article attacking Tasmania's slackness in not protecting its prime marsupial carnivore. The little animal, still a nonentity in the public consciousness, had now become unique and possibly endangered, yet the Board seemed careless of its welfare.

The long article is entitled 'That Devil Again', and begins with a report on an escaped devil from a New South Wales circus, refers scathingly to freezing devils in London Zoo, and concludes with a salute to a hunting magazine, *Australian Outdoors*, uncharacteristically deploring pastoral ignorance of Tasmania's unique little carnivore.

The article's centrepiece, however, is the reproduction of a lengthy letter written to Guiler by Thistle Y. Stead, the Society's Honorary Secretary, who was also editor of *Australian Wild Life*. Her letter included 21 questions:

1. Is the Board conducting a survey on the distribution and population densities of the Tasmanian Devil (*Sarcophilus harrisii*)? If so, when did the survey commence; what areas have been surveyed; and how many investigators are employed in the investigation?

2. Has the Board, or any member of it, published any matter concerning the distribution and population densities of the Tasmanian Devil? If so, where and when was such material published?

3. How many members of the Board are actually engaged in field research and have an intimate knowledge of the Tasmanian Devil in its wild state? What are the names of the members claiming such knowledge?

4. Has the Board made public any knowledge that it may possess on the distribution and population densities of the Tasmanian Devil through the Tasmanian Press or through questions asked in Parliament? Has it made public such knowledge in any other manner?

5. Has the Board made the public aware that though Tasmanian devils and other wholly protected fauna may be accidentally trapped, that it is ILLEGAL on the part of the trapper to transfer such animals as are trapped to places where they may be artificially confined under conditions opposite to their natural environment? If the Board has made this matter apparent to the public, by what means was it made apparent, and has the Board's opinion on this matter been published in the Tasmanian Press? If so, when?

6. In view of the obvious trend of the Tasmanian public against zoos, does the Board intend to issue further permits for the establishment of further zoos?

7. How many permits have been issued by the Board for zoos in Tasmania in the last 21 years? How many zoos

are extant; and what are the precise localities in which
they are extant; and what are the names of the holders
of the permits?

8. In view of the national trend against trading and trafficking
in wild life, does the Board intend to issue further permits
to individuals likely to engage in such traffic?

9. How many permits have been issued by the Board for the
export of Tasmanian Devils to all sources; and precisely
how many Devils have been exported in the past 21 years?

10. In what year were the most Devils exported?

11. In instances where the Board issues permits to wild life
traders or persons engaged in the exhibition or traffic of
wild life—does the Board charge a fee for such permits?
Has the Board fixed any limit to what may be paid or
received in transactions dealing with the sale of Tasmanian
Devils? If so, what is the monetary difference between the
fee charged and the profit made by the individual trader?
If so, how much is the fee for such a permit? If not—to the
aforementioned—why are permits issued to individuals to
possess wild life which is public property? Does the Board
agree or not agree that a negative view is antipathetic to
the purpose for which the Board was created?

12. Does the Board issue permits for the destruction of
Tasmanian Devils which are public property, gratis—
or is a fee charged? If a fee is charged for a permit, what
is the monetary difference between the value of the fee,
and the cost of inspection to the public to establish
the rightness of the permit? If a fee is not charged,
why is it not?

13. How many permits have been issued by the Board for the
destruction of Tasmanian Devils since 1957?

14. Does the Board require the holders of permits for the

destruction of Tasmanian Devils to return to the Board the numbers of animals destroyed? If not, why not?

15. In view of the scientific value of destroyed Tasmanian Devils, has the Board made provision to see that such specimens are not wasted? Is there a legal obligation on the part of permit holders to return destroyed animals to the Board?

    (The WILD LIFE, PRES. SOC. of AUST. is vitally concerned with this question in view of the thoughtless wastage of destroyed thylacines in the past, and the consequent rarity of both skeletal and anatomical material, which, for the most part is housed in foreign institutions. It is strongly urged that such a situation should not be permitted to occur in respect of *Sarcophilus*.)

16. Is the Board able to name Australian scientific institutions which have benefited by donations of specimens of *Sarcophilus*? If so, how many institutions have received such donations through the Board?

17. Is the Board able to name foreign institutions which have benefited by donations of specimens of *Sarcophilus*? If so, how many donations have been made in the past 21 years, and what are the names of the recipient institutions?

18. In connection with the press statement made recently by the Chairman of the Board concerning the alleged destruction by Tasmanian Devils at Bridport, would the Board state how many permits for the destruction of this marsupial have been issued to date, and how many animals have been destroyed?

19. Similarly, would the Board state how many permits it has issued for the destruction of Tasmanian Devils during the past three years at or near the following Tasmanian townships: . . . (a) Temma, (b) Marawah, (c) Trowutta,

(d) Redpa, (e) Christmas Hills, (f) Mole Creek,
(g) Bridport, (h) Hamilton?

20. Is the Board able to state what may be favourable
    variations in *Sarcophilus* tending towards its survival in
    satisfactory numbers? Similarly, is the Board able to state
    what may be unfavourable variations tending otherwise?

21. To state that one species of mammal is 'as common as any
    other marsupial' is too vague for an empirical and analytic
    appreciation of a species population disposition and position.
    Would the Board state more precisely the numerical
    relationship of the Tasmanian Devil to other marsupials?[6]

Guiler commenced his research less than three years later and
it is likely this correspondence provided some impetus for it,
given the apparent lack of official and scientific interest in devils
at that time.

Australian Outdoors, a classic hunting and fishing magazine
complete with advertisements for the latest firearms, boats and
fishing tackle, ran an article in its November 1961 issue entitled
'Protection That Doesn't Protect'. The 3000-word article, by
Jack Bauer, attacked Tasmania's farmers and graziers, accusing
them of endangering the devil's future. Bauer wrote with impressive understanding of the animal, based on personal experience,
and it is likely that this was the first non-scientific published
account detailing the ecology and behaviour of the animal in the
wild. (Bauer noted that: 'There is very little known about the
animal. The only reliable information on this animal is given by
[Ellis] Troughton in his classic *Furred Animals of Australia*
[1941]. He gives 58 lines on this animal. Not much to go by.')[7]

Bauer's article led with praise for the protected status of the
devil, while deploring the agricultural sector for branding it a

ferocious killer of poultry and lambs. A farming group or groups had apparently been pushing the scare for some two years, and had now warned that if left unchecked the devil would become as great a menace as the dingo was on the mainland. Bauer insisted that those farmers were quite wrong, and that he had scientific proof to back him up. Proof from who? None other than Dr Eric Guiler of the Zoology Department, University of Tasmania.

Guiler had recently conducted a study of the stomach contents of eighteen devils captured in southern Tasmania, a heavily farmed part of the state. Only two had eaten wool. Yet *Australian Wild Life*, in commending the Bauer article, and quoting selectively from it, did not mention its nemesis Guiler and his central role in making the Bauer case possible.

Bauer's empirical observations are many, including those derived from a long vigil he kept observing a devil lair. He took photos, which he called the first ever of the animal in its native habitat. Accompanying one of these is a caption which is as good a description as any of the devil: 'Note his long nose, tough body and sturdy legs. He's made for travelling rough in scrub terrain'.[8]

Jack Bauer's 'Protection That Doesn't Protect', an important historical document, is reproduced here in full:

This is a unique animal, a sort of living link between high marsupials and the most primitive of all. Once it lived on the mainland from which it seems to have vanished. Today it is making its last stand, its last fight for survival, in Tasmania, and in all the world there is only 26 215 square miles left to it.

But even in such a small part of the world as this the Tasmanian devil, *Sarcophilus*, is encountering an ignorance which could exterminate it. Zoologists and government experts are unanimous that the devil fully justifies the Protected Animal tag it wears but for the last two years many Tasmanian farmers and graziers have claimed it to be a ferocious poultry and lamb killer. 'Give us permits to kill him in traps or with poison' they clamor. Recently some farmers gave the press this statement, which embodies a kind of death sentence for the devil.

They wrote: 'The devil has been attacking lambs and poultry. Wombats are also disappearing. Unless something is done about the devil now, it could become as much a menace as the dingo is on the mainland.'

These gentlemen apparently cannot tell the difference between a devil and a dingo. The devil is just about the size of a terrier. The dingo is a non-marsupial and consequently has a much higher IQ than the devil. The rate of mortality at birth must be much greater in the marsupial devil whose birth is a harder and more precarious one than that of the dingo. It was probably the dingo that contrived to exterminate or deplete the devil family in the mainland. There are about 200 dingoes to every devil.

The farmers' statement was followed by another one from Dr Guiler of the Zoology Department, University of Tasmania. He said: 'The devil is rarely found in the southern regions. But recently 18 devils were captured and sent to me at the university and examination of their stomach contents showed that only two of them had eaten wool.'

Thus it appears that the devil will occasionally take a lamb but in the country in which it lives it finds it easier to take smaller marsupials, wombats, bettongs, potorus and the extremely prolific Thylogales or scrub wallabies. However some thoughtless farmers and graziers are killing devils on their properties. Yet how many lambs do they lose to the devils! How do they know that the few lambs that they lose are actually killed by devils? Unless they see devils in the act of killing their livestock they cannot be sure that these animals are the killers.

Tracks don't mean a thing in the rough, scrubby and rocky bush in which these graziers' sheep roam. As to poultry kills, these can be blamed on domestic cats gone wild which are very plentiful in most parts of Tasmania. Likewise, the native cats may be the killers. And wedge-tail eagles, crows and hawks may account for some lambs too.

There is very little known about the animal. The only reliable information on this animal is given by Troughton in his classic *Furred Animals of Australia.* He gives 58 lines on this animal. Not much to go by, but not much for farmers and graziers to pin killings on the devil.

The first record of its existence comes from Deputy Surveyor Robert Harris who in 1808 wrote: 'These animals were very common . . .'

It was probably its devilish appearance that earned it the present monicker. The adjective 'Tasmanian' was added when it was found that it lived only in Tasmania.

But does it really? Here is something that will put doubts in your mind. Mr Troughton writes: 'A devil was killed at Tooborac about sixty miles from Melbourne in 1912 which may possibly have escaped from the zoo or private captivity . . . Fossil remains have been discovered in other parts of Australia. The recent appearance of skulls found in various localities in Victoria, including portions found amongst bones of existing marsupials in a kitchen midden of the aborigines supports the view that it may still exist there.'

Thus the 'Tasmanian' devil should be regarded as an Australian animal, an animal that may exist or not in the mainland but which is of the utmost importance to all nature lovers and outdoorsmen. It has been classified in the subfamily Dasyurinae which includes all our marsupial predators, ie, native cats, tiger cats, the Tasmanian tiger (here again there is ample proof that this 'Tasmanian' animal lived in the mainland in ancient times from where it may have been exterminated by the more developed dingo when this was introduced here by aborigines or Asian peoples many thousands of years ago) and the mysterious Striped-Marsupial Cat of North Queensland which appears to be no ghost but a reality.

These predators are in a way relations of the American possums which are also marsupial and carnivorous but are tree-dwellers whereas our Dasyurus, except for the tiger cat, are ground dwellers. Thus the devil along with the native cat and the Tasmanian tiger or Thylacine, *is the only ground-dwelling marsupial predator on earth. If it became extinct a whole animal species would disappear from the face of the earth.* Do you now realise its importance?

The thoughtless, meat-hungry early settlers of Tasmania contrived to exterminate the island's emu, almost blotted out the Forester kangaroo (it is wholly protected but its numbers are small) and managed to practically exterminate the Thylacine or Tasmanian tiger. They also poisoned, shot and trapped hundreds of devils before these animals became protected. Together with the settlers' slaughter a strange disease which has not been explained, seems to have attacked the members of the Dasyurinae in Tasmania some 50 years ago.

[All] Of a sudden, the outback people and the naturalists of the day realised that these animals had become rare and that some—like the tiger—seemed to have disappeared. What happened to them? Nobody knows. And that's why scientists are most concerned with the fate of the devil. For some reasons these primitive marsupials seem to have it harder to survive these days. And the devils have been able to survive in Tasmania possibly because there are no dingoes here. Nor are there any foxes. Thus the devils—and the Thylacines— have no competition.

In four years in Tasmania I have encountered exactly 11 devils in the bush and have spent many hours observing three in captivity. From my observations I have concluded that it is almost impossible to establish exactly what is devil habitat. I have encountered devils in the rainforests of the Cradle Mountain Lake St Clair Reserve in the West Coast of the island. I have seen one on the tea-tree and gum bush along the Crotty Track also in the West Coast This part of the island has a very heavy rainfall. But I have seen devils around the drier, scrubby, rocky bush around Table Mountain, Central Tasmania and also in the high, bleak country around the Arthur Lakes.

Thus it looks like the devil has a wide range in the island, but I feel that his favorite habitat must be country of dense bush. He doesn't look like a 'savannah animal', a runner. He isn't a fast runner. Dogs can easily overtake him.

He is essentially a scrub animal. Physically he seems just made for the scrub country. His compact, tough body, his short legs are assets for him to run through brush and to crawl under logs and into hollow trees. As far as I know he isn't a tree-climber. But I do know that he is a very silent mover, another asset for him to hunt in scrub country and to approach his quarry silently.

It is always jet black with some spots or stripes on different parts of the body. Some I have seen had only one stripe across the throat, others had one or two spots on different parts of the body. Mainly, he is all black, though. And his color is an excellent camouflage in the scrub. Placing a black rag amongst

In the 1960s naturalist Jack Bauer spent long periods in the Tasmanian bush observing the devil. One night encounter took place near Damper Inn on the Port Davey track in far south-west Tasmania. (Photograph of Geoff Hood by Leo Luckman, Hobart Walking Club, 1940. Courtesy TMAG.)

some fallen logs I have failed to spot it from a distance. This same black rag could hardly be seen in the deep shadows of rainforests. It was also almost invisible from a distance in a stand of tea-tree gum and dogwood. Moreover, at night the devil's black coat must render him almost invisible.

They will tell you he is a 'nocturnal animal' but strangely enough of the 11 I have seen in their wild habitat only one was out at night, at 2.20 am near Damper Inn, on the Port Davey track. If the devil preys on bettongs, wombats, potorus, scrub wallabies, etc, he must go hunting toward evening and in the early morning which are the times when these small marsupials are at their feeding or watering places.

Whether or not the devil and his quarry continue to roam about the bush all night through I don't know. I have spent many nights sitting it out in the bush with a spotlight in order to spot game. All I have seen were possums, bandicoots, an occasional scrub wallaby. Except for that one devil I have mentioned.

Observing three captive devils I noted that they spend a great part of the day slumbering in their cage. These devils are a mother and her two young, a 'gal' and a 'boy'. During the day they *always* sleep bunched up together or even one on top of another but never separated. Toward evening they wake up and begin to prowl around the cage snarling and growling. Each is a prime animal and eats one rabbit a day . . .

Devils don't make good pets, but they aren't dangerous animals either. The friend of mine who keeps three in captivity has never been able to chum up with the little devils. He can handle the females. They'll never attempt to bite him. But they don't show any affection either. But he is quite unable to put a hand on the male. He's a real tough guy. As soon as my friend enters the cage, the devil snarls and shows his fangs. But he is a small animal weighing at most 12 lb (this is the weight of a prime specimen) and he can be put out of circulation with a well-placed kick if he decides to attack.

Devils smell. I have struck two devil lairs (just a scrub-bed under a log) and the smell coming from them was appalling. Like all the other Dasyurus, the female devil's pouch is oriented backwards, that is, contrariwise to the kangaroo's. She seems to have a usual litter of two young which she carries in the pouch for perhaps three months or so. In the pouch there are two pairs of teats.

In the old days, devils were killed by dogs, shot by hunters, poisoned, and trapped. As you can imagine, shooting a devil is no great shakes as a sport but you do have to shoot quickly because although he is a slow runner, he can move plenty fast in the scrub. He moves in a lop-sided, shambling gait reminiscent of a bear.

In the kangaroo-snaring boom, some years ago, many devils were caught in the snares but they didn't stay caught for long. They chewed up the string and got themselves free again. They couldn't, of course, get away from a dingo trap, in which many were caught.

To see devils in their native habitat is not easy. Much depends on luck but a great deal depends on bushcraft also. First off, watch for droppings. A devil's droppings are about the size of a possum's but when crushed the devil's always contains some bones, feathers or hair, the result of eating flesh, whereas the herbivorous possum's dung contains only vegetable matter. The droppings of native and tiger cats are smaller. However, you may find droppings and still be far from finding a devil. How far does he range? I don't know. He may be here today and ten miles away tomorrow.

Hunting kangaroos with dogs is perhaps the easiest way to see devils. The dogs often flush them out of their hiding places. That's just what happened a few weeks ago when our dogs roused a devil from under a log in Central Tasmania. We let the little chap get away then I went to inspect the log. Just under it and completely hidden from sight, was his lair, a scrub bed badly matted with droppings and badly stinking. Nobody had ever taken pictures of a wild devil in his native habitat and here I had the chance.

A week later I was back there. I chose a hiding place about 250 yards from the devil's lair and watched it with a pair of binoculars. About 6 o'clock in the evening just at sunset, I spotted the animal emerging from his 'home' and hitting the hunting trail. I spotted him again at dawn the next morning. That afternoon—my second day there—I made my first preparations for pictures.

With the wind blowing against my face (just the way I wanted to make sure that he was still in those parts, the devil's nose) I approached cautiously his lair and began building a hide. I was cutting a pole with my jungle-knife when I heard a noise and looking saw the devil legging it away from those parts. He'd heard or scented me and decided to beat it. That was okay with me. I built my hide from natural vegetation about 20ft away from the devil's lair under the log. Then I shouldered my pack and made tracks for home.

A week later I went back there. By this time I hoped that the devil had recovered from the scare I gave him and had become familiar with my hide as well. However, I wanted to make sure that he was still in those parts. So that evening found me in a hiding place with my binoculars. Sure enough, roundabout sunset the animal emerged from the log and hit the hunting trail. As soon as he'd gone I took my camera with tele-lens and tripod, a thermos of coffee and some sandwiches and sneaked into my hide.

I had no intention of photographing him with flashlight because I was sure I'd spook him away from those parts. So I made myself comfortable in the hide and went to sleep. I am sure I heard him return to his lair some time in the night but it might have been the noise of a roo or of the wind I heard instead. The wind, by the way, was blowing hard into my face.

It was exactly 6.10 am by my watch when my heart almost skipped a beat as I crouched over my camera tripod inside the hide. I could just see the devil's head peering over his log. I made a telephoto picture. The click of the release button didn't seem to spook the animal. Perhaps he hadn't heard it. The wind was making plenty of noise.

Gingerly he clambered over the log and for a few minutes moved restlessly about the low scrub, his sharp-pointed nose sniffing the air on which he perhaps detected some suspicious smell. Mine. But the wind was being a great help to me. I made 17 pictures of the animal showing his various reactions before he finally hit the hunting trail, moving away in that bear-like gait that makes him look so clumsy and slow. So I had obtained the first pictures ever taken of a devil in his native habitat.

From my observations it looks like that animal—at least when I was there—left his lair at dusk, returned some time during the night and went hunting at dawn again. He probably returned shortly after sunrise. These times coincide with the feeding times of most ground marsupials. However, I should have had to spend several more days in that spot to gather more accurate information. But I couldn't spare any more days.

Let me hope that my great-grandchildren will also be able to see and to photograph this fascinating little animal, which represents one solitary species living on this earth. More than any other member of our fauna does the devil need to be wholly protected. So let us hope that the Tasmanian wild life authorities will not allow farmers to destroy these animals and let us also hope that all sportsmen and outdoorsmen who know of farmers who kill devils will report them to the game inspectors or police officers. A person killing a devil can be fined up to £100 [stg] and that is really a cheap price to pay for this offence.[9]

Bipedal young devil and wolverine—the similarities in these unrelated mammals are striking. (Wolverine: Daniel J. Cox, Natural Exposures Inc. Tasmanian devil: Christo Baars)

🐾 Opposite page: *A young adult devil. This backlit photograph was taken in the wild.* (Christo Baars)

🐾 This page: *A pair of adults establish the feeding hierarchy at a food site.* (Christo Baars)
Feeding devils assess the approach of a newcomer. (Nick Mooney)

❧ King's Run. On the isolated coast of north-west Tasmania, this small shack —Geoff King's 'devil restaurant' —has played host to devil watchers from all over the world. Devils are attracted to a staked out, spotlit wallaby carcass. (Tim Dub)

🐾 *Ollie and Donny. Donny and Clyde were orphans raised at the home of David Pemberton, his partner Rosemary Gales and their children Sam, Elsa and Ollie.* (David Pemberton)

🐾 *Taz, the indomitable Warner Bros. character. Just five Taz cartoons were made between 1954 and 1964. He was resurrected in 1990 and became a billion-dollar income generator for Warner Bros.* (Courtesy Warner Bros. Taz, Tasmanian Devil and all related characters and elements are trademarks of and © Warner Bros. Entertainment Inc.)

🐾 *Aboriginal students at Rokeby Primary School in southern Tasmania wrote and illustrated a Tasmanian devil story in the tradition of Dreamtime legends.* (Courtesy Grant Williams, Rokeby Primary School)

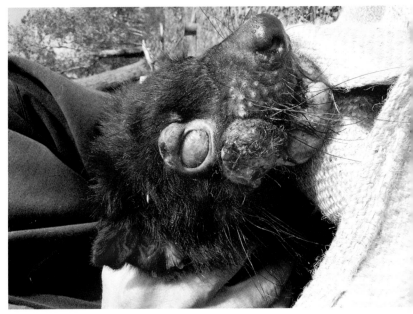

🐾 *Devil Facial Tumour Disease is a virulent cancer of unknown origin and with no known cure. First detected in 1996, it has spread across most of the island, greatly reducing the devil population in some areas and threatening the survival of the species.* (Nick Mooney)

🐾 *Albino devils are extremely rare. This photograph of one crossing a road was taken near Marrawah.* (Geoff King)

This devil, named Coolah, lived at Fort Wayne Children's Zoo in northern Indiana, United States. He had the distinction of being probably the world's oldest captive devil, living for seven and a half years, and was the last known captive devil outside Australia. (Courtesy Elaine Kirchner, Fort Wayne Children's Zoo)

🐾 *Eric Guiler initiated modern research into the Tasmanian devil; he is seen here enticing a devil to 'sing'. He also devoted much of his career to searching for the thylacine.*
(Courtesy *The Mercury*)

🐾 *A devil den and latrine site at the base of a sandstone cliff at Fentonbery. High quality dens such as this probably remain in use for hundreds of years.* (Courtesy Billie Lazenby)

7 FROM ANTICHRIST TO AMBASSADOR

In the late 1960s years we saw very few Tasmanian devils at the shack but then their population increased greatly . . . We were frequently accosted as we went out to the toilet. The children used to be quite scared of them and would come running back inside for an adult to accompany them . . . The devils became bolder and would remove items from the back porch: on one occasion they took a box of six-inch nails and we followed the trail of nails down to the beach where they had dumped the box.

JENNY NURSE, HOWRAH

In the early 1960s there weren't many Jack Bauers, or Eric Guilers. It took the stubbornness and certainty of their kind to recast the Tasmanian devil, as Mary Roberts had half a century earlier, as an animal quite unlike the popular perception of it. At Granville Harbour Guiler and his colleagues worked in tough conditions, camping in rough terrain for up to ten days, setting baited, drop-door wire cage traps in rainforest, gullies, cleared farm paddocks, coastal scrub and dune formations. The rainy, soggy, windy, cold locality had been chosen for its inaccessibility and lack of human activity; just three people lived at the harbour, with the nearest township, Zeehan, a day's drive away on a rough track.

Among Guiler's findings over the ten years of the survey: devils have a home range but do not defend territory; they use well-defined tracks and livestock trails; they travel extensively in search of food; despite the adults being solitary, they may develop some form of social intercourse at a 'general mixing area';[1] few live beyond six years; a population may fluctuate rapidly and substantially, linked to both high juvenile mortality rates and the degree of immigration of animals into an area; devils in the west are smaller than elsewhere.

A sharp, sustained increase in numbers was recorded in the latter years of the survey, beginning 'very substantially' in 1973, with the boosted population showing 'a good balance between the old, mature, and juvenile weight groups'.[2] That balance had disappeared by 1975, and many animals, when captured in 1975, weighed less. Guiler speculated that this was due to a food shortage, although 'there was no field evidence that this was in fact so'.[3] An increased population in one area would surely mean less food for all, and animals would soon lose condition, negatively affecting reproduction ability—a possible mechanism for self-correcting population imbalances.

Guiler had earlier concluded that the rising devil population might have peaked by 1969. Devil numbers and population dynamics are still not understood, despite decades of study. This lack of knowledge is hindering efforts to second-guess and possibly contain the disease that has spread across the island.

Anecdotal population evidence, in the form of newspaper accounts, is one source of information, but it is patchy, inconclusive, and open to interpretation.

In the winter of 1966, possum hunters across a small area of the midlands reported great increases in devils robbing their snares. This was put down to a rise in their numbers. The devils 'appeared to be very ravenous, according to hunters'.[4]

That behaviour suggests either a lack of food, or more vigorous competition through an increased devil population, a natural winter result of weaned juveniles. To muddy the picture further, possums were apparently more plentiful than usual in the eastern area but scarce in the western area. What, then, caused an apparently isolated outbreak of atypical behaviour?

In 1972 the same area appeared to be afflicted again, though this time farmers were the victims. 'It is believed that the animals have increased so much in the timbered country that they are venturing into the open lowlands in search of food. Some farmers are becoming concerned that they could eventually attack stock.'[5] 'Evidence' for this included the discovery of a devil hiding behind a deep-freeze unit in a garage in Oatlands.

A dramatic report then declared:

Devils loom as menace . . . Tasmanian devils had recently attacked chained farm dogs, a spokesman for the Tasmanian Farmers, Stockowners and Orchardists' Association [TFSOA] claimed yesterday. They had savaged domestic animals and had been found inside at least two farm houses. 'The build-up in the population of this dangerous pest is alarming', the president of the TFSOA (Mr R. J. Downie) said. 'We are getting reports which strongly suggest a population explosion among devils. They are being reported from places where previously devils were unknown, or at least, not a problem. They are readily attacking stock, prowling around and in farm buildings, and fighting with chained farm dogs,' Mr Downie said.[6]

The president went on to say that his association recognised the role of native fauna and would never advocate their mass destruction; but there is little doubt that his awareness of the devil being something of its own advocate—a threat while a boon—came from Dr Guiler, who had not long before warned farmers that, 'a permit [to destroy devils] is the last line of defence. It is a recognition of failure to keep pastures clean and free from dead animals. A buildup of devils to plague proportions can only occur if food is available. In this respect the devil takes advantage of man's untidy habits'.[7]

The difficulty with such accounts is in knowing what to believe. An island-wide increase would surely have been commented on elsewhere. Yet what conditions might create a purely 'local' increase? Food supply—including dead and vulnerable sheep and cows—plays a part.

For fifteen years no more was heard of the devil as a problem, but in 1987 another population surge made it newsworthy again. Launceston's daily newspaper the *Examiner* kicked off:

Farmers down Cranbrook way are having a devil of a time, and would like the power to legally do something about it. The small east coast district is beset with Tasmanian devils, but as a wholly protected animal the ferocious little marsupials can maraud hen houses with the full protection of the law . . .
A farmer's first concern is for his stock, so when someone or something is crunching his critters his instinct is to shoot first

and ask questions afterwards . . . Although local folk agreed
that an unusually and annoyingly large number of devils
had been roaming the district lately, most thought the word
'plague' was a bit too strong. 'They're a pest, not a plague',
said Jim Amos, of Cranbrook House, who has lived and farmed
there all his 70-odd years. A story in yesterday's *Melbourne Sun*
told how 'a plague of voracious Tasmanian devils is causing
havoc on the east coast' . . . Merino stud farmer Geoff Lyne
claimed to have lost 75 ducks and 50 hens to the little devils in
the last few months, [they] had attacked ewes during lambing
and savaged a $2000 ram as it lay trapped in an irrigation
ditch . . . Most farmers and townsfolk had lost chooks to the
mean marsupials, but Mr Amos said that devil numbers had
been up for 15 years, and he had even had them living under
his house. 'They're like possums now—they're dead on the
road all the way to Swansea.' Mrs Ethel Poole, 72, of
Cranbrook, said that devils had carried off all but two of her
chooks. 'They're thick as fleas around here, and they're sly
things—they left me with two old boilers,' she laughed.[8]

In June 1987 the rural *Tasmanian Country* took a less light-
hearted view:

Farmers in Tasmania's North-East are concerned about large
numbers of Tasmanian devils in the area. While the devils are
causing problems with livestock, the farmers are at a loss to
know what steps can be taken about what they consider to be
plague proportions of the wholly protected native animals . . .
Waterhouse farmers, Lindsay and Lois Hall, say they can barely
set foot outside their back door without running into devils.
Mrs Hall said that 25 years ago she would see 'the odd one'.
However, she said, on their cattle grazing property, large
numbers were now seen during the daytime and were creating

havoc. Mrs Hall said the Tasmanian devils took their chickens and ducks and chewed the ears and tails off newborn calves if they were too slow to stand up. She said the devils had also been known to take a litter of pups.

Mrs Hall said she believed the problem started when, about six years ago, large numbers of Tasmanian devils were brought to the area from Cape Portland where they were becoming a nuisance. Since then they had bred up to plague proportions. Mrs Hall believes because there were so many Tasmanian devils in the area there was a shortage of food and the animals were in poor condition and mangy. 'I wouldn't like to see them go because they are a unique animal,' she said.[9]

Mrs Hall's sympathy for the devil was admirable, given the dislike of it held by many in rural industries. But a few others were beginning to see a different value in the animal. A metamorphosis, dollar-inspired though it may have been, had begun back in the mid-seventies when a prominent businessman and

The official logo of the Tasmania Parks & Wildlife Service. (Used with permission of and © the Tasmania Parks & Wildlife Service)

member of the then Tasmanian Tourist Authority suggested that the devil be used to attract tourists. A sixteen-week global study trip had shown him:

> Tasmania is almost unheard of throughout the world, and those who know of our State, know it only because of its connection with the Tasmanian devil . . . Now is the time for us to sell, sell, sell our natural product through our tourist industry . . . Many parts of the world are suffering from the thoughtlessness that has accompanied industrial expansion, and we must do everything we can to preserve our unspoiled environment.[10]

Luring tourists to a place for its wildlife is understandable. Taking an animal out of its natural habitat to attract tourists to that place is a different matter. So it was that in 1981 the Tasmanian government proposed to use a devil as a central feature of a tourism task force visiting New Zealand. The animal would then be donated to a university for scientific study. It's hard to imagine a lone devil in a cage enticing anyone to visit its homeland, and the Australian government in any event refused an export license. When this failed, donation became the next option, and attention turned to Japan.

The State government found a way around the issue, donating four devils to Osaka Zoo in 1984. According to the official ministerial news release, they were being given

> to the Japanese people . . . The gift of the devils will help to cement the bonds which are being developed between Tasmania and Japan . . . The devils will be unusual but important ambassadors for our State . . . The Japanese people were fascinated by the devils, and their interest in the animals would focus attention on Tasmania. The Japanese press had

already given extensive coverage to the pending arrival of the animals, describing them as the 'strangest of all animals' and 'with strong teeth, even to bend iron stick' . . . Osaka Zoo officials had prepared a special home for the devils, and plans also were being made for an official receiving ceremony.[11]

A few years later three more devils, the youthful Mo, Mavis and Mary, were presented to the Sapporo Maruyama Zoo in Japan's Hokkaido state. The Tasmanian official accompanying them on the flight, Ray Groom, the Minister for Forests, Mines and Sea Fisheries, expressed the hope that they would breed in captivity, again 'putting Tassie in the spotlight'.[12] Needless to say, they didn't breed, but as a marketing ploy it worked; the devil was to become as significant as the koala as an iconic Australian image.

This new-found respect for the animal in its home state was not before time. While devils continued to be regarded as pests in some agricultural areas, public sensitivity to its status rebounded on the university, which since the time of Flynn had been associated with research for its protection. A saga which made international news in 1985 started with a front-page report in *The Mercury* headlined 'Uni's Devilish Experiments Anger Animal Libbers':

Animal Liberationists have warned they will picket and possibly invade a University of Tasmania seminar in Hobart tomorrow to protest against experimentation on and slaughtering of at least 11 Tasmanian devils. The seminar, in the university's zoology department, has been arranged for the presentation of reports on research to ascertain the temperature regulation of Tasmanian devils' brains.

The experiments were by an honours student working on

his Bachelor of Science honours thesis. A spokesman for the Tasmanian chapter of Animal Liberation, Mrs Pam Clarke, yesterday said the experiments had been futile. Several animals which had had sensitive temperature recording instruments called thermocouples implanted in their brains had been found to be useless for the experiments because the thermocouples had corroded. 'The devils, a part of our unique wild fauna, have been through a horrendous series of experiments,' she said. 'We were horrified to read that many of them died during the implantation operations and also during other experiments,' she said.

The survivors had been forced into prolonged exercise on an enclosed treadmill. An electric shock grid had been put at the rear of the treadmill 'to encourage the animals to continue running', but this was discontinued because 'it caused unnatural responses and also affected the chart recorder'.

Mrs Clarke said the distressed devils had suffered substantial injuries to their tails and paws when caught between the treadmill and the boundary wall. Animal Liberation also has claimed that an unspecified number of native cats and possums have been slaughtered in university-sanctioned experiments. 'Animal Liberation calls on the university to open its doors on the secrecy surrounding animal experimentation and appoint a member of an animal welfare organisation to its animal ethics committee,' Mrs Clarke said.

The head of the pathology department in the university's medical faculty, Prof Konrad Muller, yesterday defended the experiments on the grounds that the research was important. A similar appraisal of another animal's brain, for instance a rabbit's, would not have given the desired results. The 11 Tasmanian devils had been ordered by Dr S. C. Nicol, of the university's physiology department, with the permission of the

State National Parks and Wildlife Service. Of the 11, six had been killed and their brains immediately examined. The other five had been used in a series of tests to determine the regulation of their brain temperatures.[13]

These allegations were not met with silence. The story continued on the front page of the next day's paper:

A senior lecturer at the University of Tasmania yesterday lashed out at what he called ignorant and ill-informed criticism of experiments . . . they had considerable scientific merit and had resulted in the discovery of a blood cell which controlled the temperature of the marsupial's brain. 'The experiments have a number of implications to the evolution of marsupials and the evolution of mechanisms which keep body temperature constant in all mammals, and for understanding the devil's way of life,' Dr Nicol [sic] said . . . He said the results had been enthusiastically received by the *Australian Journal of Zoology* and another Australian university which was doing similar experiments . . . The experiments were part of a thesis by an honours student for his bachelor of science degree. Dr Nicol said the student was not Australian, and poor expression had made the experiments appear worse than they really were . . . Dr Nicol said that [the thermocouples] had broken in their rubber casing, and were useless for the experiment, but had not caused the animals any extra discomfort. He also dismissed claims that devils had been forced to run for unnatural periods of time on a treadmill. 'The treadmill experiments involved only two animals which ran at 7 kmh . . . In the wild the animals keep this sort of speed up for hours.'[14]

A ministerial statement defended the university, which was not surprising given that the government had issued the experiment permits in the first place. The minister curiously observed that devils were in abundance, as if that overrode questions of ethical treatment of individual animals. The issue duly blew over.

Devils weren't long out of the news, however. Tasmanians awoke one morning in July 1988 to a front-page horror headline: 'Devil's Disease—State's Tough Little Ambassador Threatens Livestock'.[15]

The discovery of the deadly animal parasite *Trichinella spiralis* for the first time in Australia—in devils—had potentially disastrous national ramifications. Not only might it migrate to livestock (pigs are the main host) or to humans (causing eye and heart damage), but both Tasmania's and the country's disease-free livestock status might also be seriously jeopardised. The

Nick Mooney has for many years played a key role in the management and research of Tasmania's wildlife. (Kate Mooney)

infected devils all came from an area near iconic, isolated Cradle Mountain. How could a foreign parasite make its way there? Tourists? It was speculated that a devil or devils must have eaten an infected product, most likely illegally imported salami, because curing and smoking meat doesn't kill the worm.

Fortunately, the threat proved to be an unintentional beat-up. Sampling outside the Cradle Mountain area by Nick Mooney revealed the worm to be naturally present in about 30 per cent of the devil population. Government veterinary pathologist Dr David Obendorf confirmed that no crossover risk existed. 'Wherever you find Tasmanian devils you find the parasite but that's no reason for killing Tasmanian devils.'[16] It was a strange way to discover more about the tough little ambassador.

In the space of twelve months, in 1991 and 1992 three very different accounts of the devil were published by the world's foremost devil experts. The University of Tasmania conferred David Pemberton's doctoral thesis, 'Social organisation and behaviour of the Tasmanian devil, *Sarcophilus harrisii*'; Eric Guiler published his 28-page *The Tasmanian Devil*, which covers a year in the life cycle of the animal; and Nick Mooney's 'The Devil You Know' appeared in the Winter 1992 edition of *Leatherwood: Tasmania's Journal of Discovery*. Despite its brevity Mooney's article is one of the first genuinely informed accounts of the animal written for the general public. Mooney had been studying and interacting with devils for years; the importance of 'The Devil You Know' is its wealth of previously unpublished and logical assumptions about the animal, including:

- The demise of the thylacine probably resulted in diminished competition for, and predation on, devils. It is also reasonable to suppose that the niche of devils then expanded as it has for hyaenas as the number of lions diminished in Africa. I wonder if devils now may be of a larger range size and more predacious than before, gradually evolving to soak up the empty (or good as empty) thylacine niche.

- It is a pity that the first exotic eutherians our marsupials had to deal with were probably the very cream of that group as far as survival goes: humans, dogs, foxes, cats and rodents. For a long time this 'unfair' competition has clouded the true success of marsupialism.

- Small devils have a variety of natural competitors and predators including (previously) thylacine, people, other devils, quolls and large birds of prey. Eagles and people are probably two of the main reasons devils and many other Australian animals are nocturnal, directly to avoid predation and indirectly to minimise competition.

- Unusual items I have found in devil scats include: part of a woollen sock; a wallaby foot complete with snare; part of a dog or cat collar; 27 whole echidna quills; stock ear tags and rubber lamb 'docking' rings; head of a tiger snake; aluminium foil, plastic and Styrofoam; ring off a bird's leg; half a pencil; leather jacket (fish) spine; boobook owl foot; cigarette butt; part of a 'steelo' pot scraper. I have also had part of a leather boot and the knee of a pair of fat-stained jeans eaten after being left outside a tent (not with me in them).

- I have made some observations of sheep and lamb–devil interactions using military style 'starlight scopes'. Large devils will check out a flock by sniffing from 10–15 m. The sheep will group and face the devil, stamping their feet as their usual threat. If the sheep are all healthy and alert and no carrion or afterbirth is available the devil(s) quickly move on. Sick or injured stock attract much more attention. Healthy sheep without lambs usually ignore devils.

*The devil's varied and indiscriminate diet results in
disproportionately large scats. (Courtesy Nick Mooney)*

- Although devils use their extraordinary strength to escape
  traps they rarely use it to enter places to eat.
- The mechanism of foraging seems to be almost ceaseless
  patrolling . . . I have followed individual devils for more
  than 11 km along beaches and through the snow before
  losing their tracks.
- Human interference can be important, either by providing
  extra food or extra mortality, especially with illegal

poisoning. Often, as in some rural areas, it is a bit of both resulting in unusually high population turnover.[17]

Like the earlier articles by Mary Roberts and Jack Bauer, Mooney's field observations cut right through much of the dogma that continued to be associated with the devil.

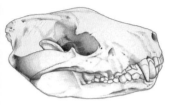

8 IN CAPTIVITY

At the devil pen the rock wall prevented my son from catching a good view, so I picked him up and we leant over for a better view. My over-priced but much-loved sunglasses fell into the pen. I contemplated retrieving them, but we then watched in awe as two devil diners crunched silently on them until they had completely devoured them. Since then I've never spent more than twenty dollars on a pair of sunglasses.

RICHARD PERRY, WEST HOBART

Tasmanian devils are easy to capture and easy to keep captive. Nocturnal by preference, devils in captivity are usually displayed during daylight and fed at optimal visiting times. They have always been regarded as curious creatures, a legacy of nineteenth-century attitudes ranking marsupials as inferior to placentals. They were displayed in zoos across the world from the mid-1800s until well into the twentieth century, when export restrictions came into place. This chapter looks at three contemporary instances of devils in captivity.

Toren Virgis is head keeper at the Bonorong Wildlife Park, not far from Hobart, which is the most visited wildlife park in

Tasmania. It is laid out to ensure maximum interaction with its wildlife. Visitors enjoy the experience of stepping around lazing kangaroos and wallabies, and many line up to be photographed with sleepy koalas, while a variety of wild parrots and wattle-birds make merry in the trees. First-time visitors might expect this tranquillity will be shattered at the devil enclosures. It never is—and for Toren Virgis that's a good thing. He is greatly concerned to strip away the myths surrounding the animal. What worries him is that it's adults who tend to need more educating than children.

A devil resting in a log den, Bonorong Wildlife Park. (Courtesy The Mercury*)*

Virgis identifies several typical visitors, including US tourists who are surprised that there is a 'real' Tasmanian devil; those who assume devils are vicious and dangerous; and a few Tasmanians who simply dislike them. Dispelling the assumption of viciousness isn't hard: most of the Bonorong devils tolerate being picked up, stroked, even tickled. Less easy to change are ingrained attitudes. A Tasmanian sheep farmer told Virgis that the sooner DFTD wiped the devils out the better. And on one occasion Virgis was educating a class of schoolchildren about devils when a boy said, 'But my dad likes to shoot them!'[1]

Bonorong's devil population averages about eight, sharing four enclosures, with larger enclosures being built for expanding numbers as a response to the disease crisis. Virgis knows his devils intimately. Thus wild-born Gunter, three years old, has a dominating, aggressive nature, and will charge screaming at the keeper, only to stop short. It's a social manoeuvre, a dominance tactic. Flash, on the other hand, born at the park, is a three-year-old male described by Virgis as a 'timid wuss'.[2] He believes this may be because Flash spent his early years with three females, who bullied him. Each devil, he says, has a distinct personality.

It took him some time to get to know them. He started at Bonorong in a part-time capacity and had been advised by a previous keeper to take a rake with him into the enclosures, to keep the devils at a distance. Virgis did this for two months. The devils didn't like it—it 'antagonised them'[3]—and neither did he. In exasperation he dispensed with the rake, got down to their level and took it from there. In the three years since, he's had just a few bites on his hands, which he calls nips, generally associated with food he's carrying.

To minimise the confinement behaviour so often associated with captive animals, such as incessant pacing, Bonorong's devil enclosures are designed to mimic natural conditions. But confinement it is, including daylight feeding and a reversal of nocturnalism and solitariness. Not that the devils seem to mind. They're treated daily to rabbit and a chicken drumstick, a supplement such as a raw egg, or mince with grated carrot or apple. The rabbit is pre-frozen to kill fleas. Virgis regularly buries food treats: devils like digging and it gives them something to do. One of those treats is 'bloodsicles', frozen cubes of blood.

The animals are rotated between enclosures for compatibility and, near mating time, as a way of finding good mate-matches. Their faeces are also rotated, again near mating time, to stimulate males into a sense of competition. In Virgis' opinion it's laziness rather than wild-latrine mimicry that has some wildlife parks leaving faeces where they are deposited.

One feature of their captive state which interests him, and that can't easily be tested in the wild, is that females tend to dominate throughout the year, except for the two-month breeding period. Then, he says, the females are 'edgy' and the males 'lose it'.[4] It is a clear case of role reversal, the males becoming highly energised, aggressive and dominating, the females submissive.

Virgis is well aware that captive breeding isn't a magic solution to the decline of the devil. He goes back to education, to attitudes, and laments in particular Tasmania's hunting culture—gun users don't only hunt for the pot. The wildlife parks are already playing a central role in combating DFTD through their greatly stepped-up breeding programs. And information comes to them: a visitor to Bonorong, a South African dentist, remarked casually to Virgis that a mystery disease killing bovines and carnivores in southern Africa, in which cancerous lesions developed about the face and mouth, had been traced to poison baiting. Virgis passed the information on to the relevant authorities. It may well come to nothing. But by the accumulation of such information difficult problems are finally solved.

Angela Anderson is resident zoologist at the Tasmanian Devil Park, a tourist attraction and wildlife rehabilitation centre at Taranna, near the Port Arthur Historic Site on the Tasman Peninsula. Anderson studied in Glasgow before taking up an internship in wildlife rehabilitation at the Wildlife Centre in Virginia, USA. There she specialised in birds of prey, treating up to 40 at a time. Across the world at the Tasmanian Devil Park a new raptor rehabilitation centre opened in 2001 and Anderson successfully applied for the position.

The Tasmanian Devil Park has a resident population of about fourteen devils. The two enclosures have sturdy metre-high walls to allow for easy viewing. However, this ease of viewing can present problems. Captive devils are inquisitive and will stand up against the inner wall, and visitors have been known to try and pat them. Children are sometimes held over the walls by their parents for a closer look, despite bold signs warning of the dangerous bite of devils. None of this is advisable. The question most frequently asked by visitors is whether they can pick one up.

On one occasion a child's parents purchased a soft toy when entering the Park. The toy was a devil, and a real devil managed to get hold of it. The child was distraught. Anderson entered the enclosure, gave chase and retrieved the toy, which was only a bit damp. This is an aspect of the animal which puzzles US visitors in particular; their expectation is that, like Taz, it has a blinding turn of speed.

Spring and early summer visitors are likely to see unweaned pups. In January 2004 one of the enclosures contained four newly independent siblings, their mother having been returned a month before to the nearby adult enclosure, and another four still with their mother because of the persistence of a late suckler. The independent four continued to display a great sense of bonding, sleeping all over each other.

The two mothers are sisters, who three years earlier had arrived at the Park as roadkill pouch-young. The adult enclosure's patriarch is seven-year-old Max, whose final litter was approaching two years in age. The Park's multiple bloodlines permit a number of breeding combinations—a captive breeding strategy that has become all the more important now that wild devils are no longer being introduced while DFTD remains rampant. It would be enormously risky to introduce a wild strain, despite the Tasman Peninsula's isolated and naturally low devil population, which is linked to the rest of the island only by a swing bridge across a manmade canal at Dunalley.

Educating visitors as to the specific implications of DFTD, and of the extinction threats to so many other native species, is for Anderson a significant aspect of the Park's role. Anderson is a great admirer of devils. For her, they are 'very shy. The devils we have were reared by their parents or brought in from the wild and we've never had any problems with them at all. The only devils that I have seen to be aggressive are the ones that were hand-reared. They've got no fear of humans'.[5] She can attest to this. Once she was in an enclosure bending down to get a water bowl when a devil that had been hand-reared latched on to her shin. She shook it off by leaping out of the enclosure but has a scar as a permanent reminder of the incident.

Foraging behaviour is encouraged through varying types and amounts of food. On one day a number of small pieces will be tossed into the enclosure; on another it may be just one large piece for them to wrestle over. Two or more devils tugging at a chunk of meat and bone may look like competitive feeding but it is in fact cooperative, because in this way the food is quickly broken into manageable pieces.

An innovative, and energetic, feeding method is the suspension of meat on a bungee cord for the animals to leap at. Meat pieces are also hidden about the enclosures, in cardboard boxes and in toilet roll centres. Roadkill, generally wallaby, makes up a large proportion of the food, along with laboratory rats, and

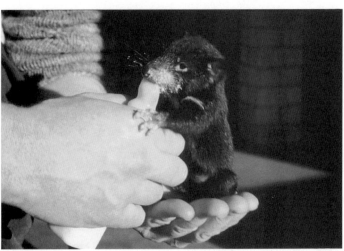

Live baby devils are frequently found in the pouches of their roadkilled or disease-killed mothers. They are kept in captivity by human carers (to whom they readily take) until old enough to fend for themselves in the wild. (Courtesy Nick Mooney)

rooster carcasses from chicken farms. Devils are partial to dog biscuits and eggs. Anderson has observed a mother attempting to encourage her young from the den by running up and down outside with food in her mouth. On the other hand, there are times when the mother will take food from her young.

The two enclosures are to be replaced by a large one-acre enclosure alongside the raptor rehabilitation centre. It is to be hoped that a healthy population of devils will result for eventual breeding purposes, should DFTD continue to decimate the wild populations. And visitors will hopefully continue to be informed of the fragility of Australia's natural world and the threat to so many of its species. Anderson's silent raptors are a stark reminder of this. A pair of wedge-tailed eagles occupies an open enclosure. They can't fly. One was shot, the other flew into a powerline. A goshawk, shot through a wing, was cared for and released; the same bird was returned with a bullet through its neck and is now a permanent resident. They are a few of the many brought in for treatment. Many more continue to die, victims of cars, guns, powerlines, poisoning, trapping and domestic animals, as extinction threats rise inexorably across Tasmania and all of Australia.

Fort Wayne is a city in northern Indiana. Its story is in many ways a microcosm of US history. In 1794, after defeating the indigenous Miami peoples, General Anthony Wayne built a fort at the junction of two rivers in order to facilitate permanent white settlement. The arrival of the railroad in the 1850s significantly boosted the town. Today it's a manufacturing centre surrounded by fertile farmland, with a population of about 170 000—similar to Hobart's. Among its attractions is a children's zoo. The opening of its Australian Adventure in 1987 was the crowning event of that year. The zoo broke all attendance records, and received a prestigious award from the professional zoo community.[6]

A Tasmanian devil named Coolah became a star attraction. When Coolah died in May 2004, he was seven and a half years old: possibly the world's oldest devil. Elaine Kirchner, supervisor of the Australian Adventure, looked after Coolah throughout his life at the zoo. Her experiences were summarised in an email interview with David Owen.[7]

David Owen: You've looked after twelve devils in seventeen years—you must have a very good understanding of the nature of the animal. Do they differ much in personality? Any interesting examples of personality contrasts?

Elaine Kirchner: Tasmanian devils, like most animals, do have differences in 'personalities'. Some are very much loners and don't want anything to do with other animals. On the other hand, we had two sisters, Rosie and Kestra, that nearly always slept in the same nest box. Every few days they would move all of the nest material to a different nest box and set up housekeeping there. We generally housed our devils singly, but Rosie and Kestra were very close. The only time we mixed more than these two together was during breeding season. We have found that during most of the year the female devils are dominant. It seems that when breeding season rolls around, the males assert their importance, if only for these few days. Frequently the males will drag the females around the exhibit by the scruff of the neck. They often corner them in a nest box, not allowing them to leave for up to two or three days.

Some animals were very curious and routinely explored every corner of their exhibit each morning. Others were content to go for a run around the place and settle in to sleep.

Many years ago we moved them to an outdoor area, and then added four shelter areas for them. These were triangular, covered with brush and wood chips. All faced the public but were at various distances from the boardwalk. Some animals chose to sleep in the one closest to the public, some far away, and often an animal slept behind the shelters!

New animals in the exhibit always seem to be a challenge. When we got our two sisters in 1996, we had our assistant volunteer watch the animals to make sure they stayed in the exhibit. After about an hour or so, we heard a frantic call from Dianna saying that one of the youngsters was at the top of the fence. Dianna was armed with only a radio and a clipboard. Needless to say, all of the animal care staff moved quickly to contain the devil and modifications were immediately made to the hotwire!

David Owen: The devil's reputation for being ferocious is unfounded. But you surely must have developed a good respect for their inquisitiveness which includes a preparedness to bite. Did you have any unpleasant encounters over the years? And if so did you develop any methods to counter that instinct? And your broader interaction with them?

Elaine Kirchner: We learned over the years to have a healthy respect for all of those teeth and those strong jaws. My first encounter with an uncontained devil came early one morning, only a few weeks after we had received our first two animals from Australia. We had been told that devils don't climb, and so had them housed in holding areas built of concrete block with wooden fences. The enclosure was just over a meter in height. These animals were less than a year old and quite agile. When I arrived at work one morning, I noticed that one of the animals was not in her pen. A quick look around told the story—she was on top of our bird holding cages, way back in the corner. I quickly called the assistant director for help, he crawled up on top of the cages with a net to recapture the critter. I was in the aisleway underneath him, along with a cage housing two angry water rats. The only flaw to this plan was an unsecured piece of wire. The animal went through the hole and into the hall with me. I had no net, and no way to get to one without letting the animal escape. We chased each other around the water rat cage several times until I managed to get a cage door open and the animal went into the cage. We later learned that the folks who told us that devils don't climb had one animal who was quite old and very obese!

In general, we don't enter the enclosure with the devils. If we must, we use a large warehouse broom to keep between ourselves and the animal. They seem not to know that they can go around the ends of the broom. When we need to restrain them, we try to grab them at the base of the tail. It takes several keepers to hold one down for blood draws. Since they have virtually no neck, someone needs to have rather large and strong hands to hold down the head.

David Owen: Your website mentions devils at San Diego, Cincinnati and Toronto zoos; also a figure of some sixty devils in North America since 1983. Did Fort Wayne begin with a consignment from Australia or did you obtain captive stock from other North American zoos?

Elaine Kirchner: Eight of our animals came from Australia, the rest from North American zoos.

David Owen: I hope Coolah's enjoying his later years. What can you tell us about him?

Elaine Kirchner: Coolah is a rather small animal as devils go. He is nearly all black, just has a smallish patch of white on his rump. His teeth seem to be in pretty good shape. We do give our devils some whole prey but most of it is in chunks. They eat slices of rabbit, whole day-old chicks, fish (though he always bites off the heads), dry dog food, and the occasional meat ball. His birthdate is listed as January 1, 1997 at the Cincinnati Zoo, though I don't know if that is an actual date or an estimate. In looking at the records I just noticed that his grandfather actually lived at our zoo also for a few years at the same time Coolah was here.

Our first Tasmanian devils arrived here in June of 1987, just at the time we opened our Australian area. In 1989 we acquired four more animals from Australia, giving us a total of six.

As an older animal, Coolah does have some health issues, but still continues to hold his own. Our zoo opens for the season in a few weeks, so he'll be back in his exhibit then. Until that time he has two indoor pens and a couple outdoors as well. Just yesterday he was laying in the sun in mid-afternoon, acting like he had not a care in the world. He looks forward to his morning chick—even if it has medicine inserted inside it. Most mornings he comes out of the box to greet me, though he does like to sleep in at times. Now that it is light [early] in the mornings, he most often gets up and looks for his morning treat, though that comes a bit later.

David Owen: Finally, did you need to have much contact with Australian wildlife people?

Elaine Kirchner: I do have contact with a number of Australian zoo folks. Androo Kelley from Trowunna Wildlife Park has been a great help with devils, and actually visited us several years ago. I have worked with a number of Australian species—echidnas, wombats, dingoes, Eastern grey kangaroos, Tammar wallabies, kowari, lizards, & numerous bird species. I have hand-reared two kangaroos and a wallaby. They lived with me for up to a year and went everywhere I went—I wore them in a pouch around my neck during the day, hung them on the doorknob at night. I am a co-studbook keeper for grey kangaroos in North America, and devote a lot of time to those wonderful creatures.

Elaine Kirchner contacted David Owen not long after the conclusion of the interview, on 23 April 2004:

I need to let you know that we have unfortunately discovered that Coolah has inoperable cancer. He has a large tumor on his backside that is also infected. We will still allow him to be on display and will probably have a sign detailing his health problems. I see no reason to banish him from his exhibit just because he is ill. I will let you know how things are going with him—right now he in on an antibiotic to clear up some of the infection and some pain medication. We have done an ultrasound and brought in a couple of consulting vets.

Her next email read:

I'm sorry to have to inform you that we had to euthanize our Tasmanian devil Coolah this morning. He had an inoperable malignant tumor on his backside. We've let him enjoy the sunshine and be on exhibit when he felt like it for the past few weeks. In the past week he has stopped eating—never a good sign for a Tassie devil.[8]

9 'THE
SPINNING
ANIMAL
FROM TASMANIA'

I was lab manager in the Zoology Department at the University of Tasmania from 1962 until 1979 and I worked closely with Dr Eric Guiler. On one occasion he had at the department a number of devils in cages built into a room. Three in all, separated by steel mesh and right to the ceiling. There was one light bulb over the centre cage. Sometime during the first night the devil in that cage climbed up the mesh and chewed off the bulb and its holder. All that was left were two small pieces of electric cable sticking through a small hole in the ceiling. A good thing the light had not been left on.

RUSSELL WHEELDON, SANDY BAY

The story of how a small nocturnal marsupial carnivore came to be immortalised as a Hollywood cartoon icon is an unlikely one. It involved chance, luck, unsolved intrigue and a clutch of dramatically different personalities, among them movie mogul Jack Warner, Hollywood artist Robert McKimson, film star Errol Flynn and his father Theodore.

In 1883 a young Russian Jew, escaping the threat of Tsarist pogroms, arrived in New York. His surname may have been Varna; immigration authorities anglicised it as Warner. His wife later joined him in Baltimore where he had opened a shoe repair shop. Some ten years later their young sons, Harry, Sam, Abe and Jack, lured by the thrill and potential of nickelodeons, pooled together to buy a broken Kinetoscope projector (the silent film *The Great Train Robbery* came with it). They repaired the projector and screened the film in a tent in their backyard. So began the illustrious cinematic career of the Warner brothers.

Jack, the future all-powerful head of Warner Bros., had to wait until he turned sixteen before his brothers allowed him to become a formal partner in their grandly named Duquesne Amusement Supply Company. That was in 1909—a notable Tasmanian devil year. Thousands of kilometres west, at 42° South, Theodore Thomson Flynn and his pregnant wife Lily had just arrived in Hobart from Sydney, where he had been appointed the Ralston Professor of Biology at the University of Tasmania. (As a point of comparison, Flynn's annual salary was A\$500; the Warner brothers were together pulling in US\$2500 per week—well over five hundred times the professor's earning capacity.)

Theodore Flynn's enthusiasm for Tasmania, which was not matched by Lily's (she disliked the cold and missed her Sydney friends), soon led him into original terrestrial and marine research, some of the most important of which involved the Tasmanian devil. And Flynn is credited with being one of the first scientists to warn of the thylacine's impending extinction.

In June 1909 Lily, soon to rename herself Marelle, gave birth to their first child, Errol. Much has been written about famous Hollywood movie star Errol Flynn's relatively short, tempestuous life. The oeuvre constitutes a mass of contradictions. Even his autobiography *My Wicked, Wicked Ways* (with its devilishly named opening chapter) doesn't exactly set the record straight, disarming and uncomfortably honest though it generally is when he's not cracking jokes, many of them cheerfully libidinous. Throughout the book, however, Errol Flynn writes respectfully of his father. He admired Theodore's intellect and achievements in biology,[1] just as years later in Hollywood he admired, when not loathing, his boss Jack Warner.

At the university, Professor Flynn's duties were divided between lecturing, examination and research, part of which was a requirement to research the diseases of plants and animals. He made no mention of disease affecting any dasyurid. Within a year he had completed one of his more important papers, which today is still regarded as a standard Tasmanian devil reference text.[2]

Ranked somewhere between low soap opera and high intellectual and artistic achievement, the Flynn family saga is a compelling one, though father and son tend to be treated as different species in the literature, while Marelle is variously described as vivacious, fun-loving, cruel to Errol and incompatible with Theodore; Flynn was:

> a tall, handsome man, patient with Errol, overfond of alcohol, somewhat shabby for a distinguished professor [and] as a contrast to his wife, so full of life and gaiety, Professor Flynn was often moody and looked ill at ease in the company of others . . . wishing that he was back at his home or at the

University laboratory surrounded by his beloved animal specimens.[3]

Despite personal difficulties, including separation from Marelle, Theo went on to a career of considerable personal achievement. In 1930 he left for Belfast where until retirement he held the Chair of Zoology at Queen's University and became a member of a number of eminent societies, a far cry from the early years of bringing up naughty Errol—including the occasion Theo found himself in trouble with the Tasmanian Museum and Art Gallery from which he had borrowed skeletons of a devil, thylacines and platypuses for research purposes and not only not returned them for years but Errol had apparently damaged them.

All the while Warner Bros. Pictures Inc. was benefiting from utilising animals. Soon after setting themselves up in Hollywood the brothers began producing short serials using tame animals from a nearby zoo, in which a heroine would be 'chased' by a doddery old lion, tiger or gorilla and the serial suspended at a climactic moment until the following week. Then, in 1923, Jack Warner had the prescience—or luck—to take on a script in which a dog rescued a Canadian fur trapper (*Where the North Begins*). The search for a canine actor uncovered Rin Tin Tin, a highly trained German shepherd. The dog became Warners' first superstar, earning millions in a seven-year career. After Rin Tin Tin's death Jack kept up the animal flavour by introducing a horse, Duke, and its faithful owner, a young John Wayne. It is not surprising that Warner Bros. then took to the animated cartoon business with such gusto, since the brothers knew how positively audiences reacted to animals.

Errol Flynn refers a few times to the Tasmanian devil in his autobiography, including this (his father's?) definition:

'A Tasmanian devil (*Sarcophilus ursinus*) is a carnivorous marsupial known for its extreme ferocity'. Errol had a deep interest in the natural world from early boyhood. He loved the sea and its creatures and much of this came from Theodore, who also kept marsupials at home for research purposes. They were pleasures in a place of friction: according to Errol his mother found him unmanageable, and

> a devil in boy's clothing . . . My young, beautiful, impatient mother, with the itch to live—perhaps too much like my own— was a tempest about my ears, as I about hers. Our war deepened so that a time came when it was a matter of indifference to me whether I saw her or not . . . The *rapport* was with my father . . . When school finished, I raced home to be at his side, to hurry out into the back yard, where we had cages of specimens of rare animals. That courtyard was a fascinating place for a small boy. Tasmania is the only spot in the world where three prehistoric animals, the Tasmanian tiger, the Tasmanian devil and the animal Zyurus are found. Father had specimens of all of these in his cages, as well as kangaroo rats, opossums, sheep. I got to know these creatures very well, even the most savage, and I hated it when he had to chloroform one and dissect it . . . Occasionally I went with him on a trip in quest of one of the rare Tasmanian animals. We headed for the western coast, a difficult terrain, where there were huge fossilised trees. We hunted the Tasmanian tiger, an animal so rare it took Father four years to trap one.[4]

Errol alone knew what a Zyurus was, though he may have been relying on memory. His father had made a major palaeontological discovery in Wynyard in northwest Tasmania of the oldest known marsupial fossil, *Wynyardia bassinia*. At a nearby site was the fossil *Zygomaturus*, a wombat-like member of the megafauna.

After a period of adventuring as a young man in Australia and beyond, Errol acted in a cheap movie in England (his second) which came to the attention of Jack Warner. According to Flynn, 'Warner saw me popping around on the screen with a lot of energy.'[5] According to Jack, 'I knew we had grabbed the brass ring in our thousand-to-one-shot spin with Flynn. When you see a meteor stab the sky, or a bomb explode, or a fire sweep across a dry hillside, the picture is vivid and remains alive in your mind. So it was with Errol Flynn.'[6] The year was 1935: a wild, virile, dashing, swashbuckling Tasmanian devil had arrived in Hollywood.

Jack teamed him with the equally unknown Olivia de Havilland in *Captain Blood*. The movie made him instantly famous. Yet despite the rewards for the disgruntled, rebellious Hobart youth who'd struck the Hollywood jackpot, Errol Flynn came to begrudge as much as appreciate his luck:

> You were assumed to be Irish, your name being Flynn . . .
> Nobody knew or cared that my whole life was spent in
> Tasmania, Australia, New Guinea, England . . . Nobody
> believed me when I talked of that background. They didn't
> want to hear of it. They wanted me to be Flynn of Ireland.[7]

Still, he went on to make over 50 films, mostly with Warner Bros., until his death from a heart attack in 1959. That output of over two films a year, mostly in lead roles, is considerable, while he also found the time and energy to become the era's most colourful and controversial Hollywood identity. But he never lost his love for the sea, in particular, nor for animals. He sometimes arranged whale-watching cruises, one eminent guest being Professor Hubbs of the Scripps Oceanic Institute. He bred

Inspired by his father Theodore, Tasmanian-born actor Errol Flynn developed a lifelong devotion to animals. In the United States he was the first to breed lion hounds, also known as Rhodesian ridgebacks. The first chapter of Errol's biography is entitled 'Tasmanian Devil, 1909–1927'. (Courtesy Steve and Genene Randell, Errol Flynn Society of Tasmania, www.geocities.com/errolflynn1909)

champion lionhounds, a breed more familiarly known today as Rhodesian ridgebacks.

Flynn acrimoniously parted company with Warner Bros. in 1952, after 'a violent argument with Jack Warner . . . although we laugh at it today'.[8] And no doubt they did. In his autobiography Flynn claimed that he was one of the very few able to saunter into Warner's office and expect to be treated as an equal. Given Flynn's dominating and uncompromising personality, the outwardly gregarious Jack must have been pretty formidable himself. According to his son Jack Jr:

> [He was] the most complex and confounding of all the brothers. For years I have tried to find the keys to the labyrinth of my father's mind, but it remains now what it was throughout most of his lifetime: boxes within boxes, rooms

without doors, questions without answers, jokes without points, scenarios based on contradictions, omissions, and deceit. His was the anguished story of a man driven by fear, ambition and the quest for absolute power and control . . .[9]

It's a harsh sketch. As harsh as those caricaturing Flynn as a rapist-paedophile-Nazi. How would two such apparent demons get on in a closed room? Even Hollywood might struggle to script it . . .

Flynn's subsequent battles with drugs and legal troubles overshadowed a successful quarter-century of moviemaking and it's hard not to imagine a degree of sympathy for him from his former employer, which he had served very well. Less than two years later, in 1954 (as Flynn, in Jamaica, steadily lost his looks and highly conditioned physique), Warner Bros.' *Looney Tunes* produced a feisty, energised, crazy, ravenous, fearless, wild cartoon character, unlike any yet seen: the Tasmanian Devil.

How and why did this animated marsupial come about? There is no documentation, or official confirmation, from Warner Bros. or anyone else, linking Errol Flynn and Taz. Flynn himself makes no reference to the cartoon character in his autobiography, but just three Taz cartoons had been made when he wrote his book, and he may not even have known of their existence—back then they were a combined eighteen minutes of obscurity.

In a little under 30 years of cinema cartoon art, a host of major animated animal characters had come to life. Aimed at children (despite plenty of adult wit and sophistication), the Warner Bros. animal stars were familiar and non-threatening: Bugs Bunny, Daffy Duck, Porky Pig, Sylvester the cat and Tweety the canary, Michigan J. Frog, Speedy Gonzales the Mexican mouse, and Foghorn Leghorn the rooster. The men of

Termite Terrace (as the animation building was known) did break out of the domestic/farm mould with their skunk Pepé Le Pew in 1945 and then the ultimate chase-and-outwit duo the Road Runner and Wile E. Coyote (prompted by a wonderful personification of the coyote by Mark Twain) in 1949. All three were the creation of legendary animator Chuck Jones, already famed for Bugs Bunny.[10]

Jones and his colleagues Friz Freleng, Tex Avery, Bob Clampett and Robert McKimson were responsible for much of the 'controlled lunacy' of the *Looney Tunes* and *Merrie Melodies* output across those three decades.[11] McKimson created the Tasmanian devil (it was not then called Taz) in 1954. Why? North America has plenty of interesting and unusual wild animals. Furthermore, the real Tasmanian devil has no recognisable 'personality' and back then there was no antipodean Mark Twain to give it one—unless, of course, Errol Flynn did, through the legacy of his own dynamic, destructive, insatiable ways (three adjectives which closely fit Taz). On the other hand, McKimson had created a marsupial six years earlier, Hippety Hopper the baby kangaroo. Unlike the then-obscure devil, the kangaroo had long and famously symbolised the vast, dry Australian continent.

McKimson, whose brothers were also animators, worked with Warner Bros. for about 35 years. Jones called him 'one of the greatest',[12] and credited the series of widely used model sheets McKimson drew in the 1940s for the definitive look of the characters in the *Looney Tunes* stable. And 'in his art he was fast, he was fluid, and he was on-the-money'.[13]

There are several explanations for the origin of Taz. The most 'official' is found in the lavish *Warner Bros. Animation Art*:

Taz auteur Bob McKimson recalled that the character was born when writer Sid Marcus was 'kicking around' different types of characters. And I said, 'About the only thing we haven't used around here is a Tasmanian Devil.' He didn't even know what they were. And we just started talking about it and we came up with this character.[14]

An alternative explanation, found on a number of *Looney Tunes* fan websites, is that McKimson and Marcus created the manic creature as a new test for Bugs Bunny.

Then there is the potential Flynn link:

Desperate Journey is the first of two films in which Errol Flynn actually plays an Australian, which is what he was (Warner PR spread the word that Flynn was Irish in an effort to tone down a wild history. Then again, nobody has yet to either confirm or deny whether he was in fact the inspiration for their Looney Tunes' cartoon creation The Tasmanian Devil [aka Taz]). It is amusing to watch Flynn try to effect a mild Aussie inflection in places, but he eventually gives up and sounds like he usually does.[15]

A 1998 feature article in the *Sunday Tasmanian* produced yet another explanation. The opportunity for the article arose from a visit to Tasmania by Chuck McKimson, Robert's brother, travelling with an exhibition of Warner Bros. artwork:

Fifty-five years ago in a California art studio two brothers shared morning coffee while solving a crossword. It was a 'regular day' for Warner Bros. animators Robert and Chuck McKimson. Each morning Bob and Chuck would play teasing word puzzles. The crossword ritual primed the talented and successful siblings for a creative day inventing quirky adventures for characters such as Bugs Bunny and Daffy Duck.

One fateful morning back in 1953, Bob was solving a
word-clue referring to a spinning creature indigenous to the
Australian island state of Tasmania. Bob and Chuck, like most
Americans even today, knew little about the heart-shaped
island south of the Great Southern Land. But the McKimson
boys did know the clue's answer—the Tasmanian devil. The
question was common in 1950s crosswords. Bob and Chuck
had answered it before. 'Invariably, during that time, the clues
would mention Tasmanian devil. They wanted to know what
the spinning animal of Tasmania was', Chuck, now 83,
recalled. 'My brother, Bob, was a crossword addict and every
morning at 9 o'clock he'd sit down to do his crossword
puzzle . . . the rest of us did the same thing.'

This particular 1950s morning Bob, Chuck and their
fellow Warner Bros. animators were searching for a new

*Related? Despite the original Warner Bros. cartoon character being created in the
1950s when very little was known about the Tasmanian devil in the United States,
these images reveal some intriguing similarities between the real and the invented
animal. (Taz courtesy of Warner Bros. Taz, Tasmanian Devil and all related
characters and elements are trademarks of and © Warner Bros. Entertainment Inc.
Bipedal devil at Bonorong Wildlife Park courtesy The Mercury)*

character to play with their cool-as-a-cucumber rabbit, Bugs Bunny. 'The studio manager wanted a new character and we'd done cats and rats, horses and cows, chickens and whatever . . . so Bob says, "Let's do some research on the Tasmanian devil",'[7] Chuck said. 'So we got encyclopaedias and did some research.'

They learned the Tasmanian devil was a ferocious little creature with a legendary growl and a propensity to run around creating mayhem. 'We looked into how it behaved but there wasn't in fact too much on the Tasmanian devil in those days but whatever there was we went into it', he said. The wild creature would be an exciting counterpoint to and playmate for Bugs, and a team of about five Warner Bros. animators began sketching preliminary drawings. 'All five of us came up with an almost identical looking critter and then my brother, Bob, took those and made the final decision on what it looked like and he made the final drawing', Chuck said.[16]

And so the creature was born.[17] That first six-minute cartoon probably required about 150 story sketches, followed by up to 10 000 images painted on transparent animation cels, the whole process taking some five weeks—call it 20 working days (coincidentally about the same as the real Tasmanian devil's gestation period).

That first experimental cartoon is particularly important, for its own sake and because the 'whirling dervish'[18] very nearly didn't survive. Here is what happens in *Devil May Hare*:

The animals flee from Taz, who will devour anything and everything, past Bugs's hole, and the wily rabbit tries to bamboozle Taz with a succession of artificial animals he could try to eat. In the end, in desperation, Bugs places a Lonely Hearts ad for a female Tasmanian devil who has matrimony in mind. One flies in immediately from, presumably, Tasmania, and Bugs, in the guise of a rabbi (geddit?), marries the pair, thereby calming Taz's savage soul. (The quasi-Freudian equation of Taz's violence with a lack of sex went remarkably unremarked-upon at the time.) As the pair flies off Bugs comments: 'All the world loves a lover, but in this case we'll make an exception.'[19]

Eddie Selzer, an executive producer at Termite Terrace in 1954, objected to the new cartoon character. He thought it too violent for a junior audience, and distasteful to parents. (Warner Bros., through eldest brother Harry in the early decades, had had a strong guiding social principle, believing that cinema could and should morally educate.) Selzer didn't appear to understand the animators. Chuck Jones refers to:

> [the] twelve dreadful years of his reign . . . Perhaps his finest hour came at a story session. Four or five of us were laughing over a storyboard when once again Eddie stood vibrating at the doorway, glaring malevolently at us and our pleasure and laughter. His tiny eyes steely as half-thawed oysters, his wattles trembling like those of a deflated sea cow. 'Just what the hell,' he demanded, 'has all this laughter got to do with the making of animated cartoons?'[20]

Executive producers have power. Selzer ordered that no more devil cartoons be made. Yet someone with greater power saved Taz. Re-enter Jack Warner, who wanted the Tasmanian devil back. It was a curious decision, because that lone cartoon had seemingly been destroyed by time, never mind Selzer. Yet three years later Jack ordered his animation team to make more. And with McKimson directing, that happened—between 1957 and

1964, *Bedevilled Rabbit,* then *Ducking the Devil,* then *Bill of Hare*, then *Dr. Devil and Mr. Hare.*

Dissected by Theodore, admired by Errol, punted on by Jack, the devil almost died but was resurrected again. And the rest, as they say, is history . . .

10 OWNING THE DEVIL: TASMANIA AND WARNER BROS.

In 1960s suburban Melbourne feeding his caged devils was a problem for famed anthropologist and photographer Donald Thomson, until he found a fishmonger at the Victoria Market only too willing to give him leftover fish scraps . . . The arrangement worked well until Donald discovered that his fishmonger friend was a leading member of the Australian Communist Party. This no doubt caused some embarrassment to Donald, considering his good relationship with his other friend, Sir Robert Menzies, and Sir Robert's noted obsession with communist infiltration at that time.

JOHN TEASDALE, RUPANYUP, VIC.

Taz has no evil machinations. He is not greedy in the sense of wanting power, monetary or political, over others. He just wants to eat, by all and any means. Taz is an innocent savage. He never rose to a civilized state and then reverted. He never

fell from grace because he never had it. He has remained in a
state of nature as its most powerful force . . . He is so
outlandish as to not remind viewers of the brutes from which
they evolved. Rather, Taz makes the beast of instinct look
completely external, lovably innocent, and easy to outwit.[1]

There are tens of thousands of books about the movie
industry. Hardly any indulge in academic analysis of
animated cartoons. Yet in this short quote it is possible to reflect
on Taz the cartoon devil from perspectives of political philosophy, evolution, psychology, and cruelty in humour (we enjoy his
stupidity). But of course Taz, along with his maker, has had the
last laugh, given the amounts of money he has generated. How
did that come about?

Having lain virtually dormant for a quarter of a century, it
may seem surprising that such an apparently one-dimensional
character was selected by Warner Bros. to become a major
production of its new animation studio. In 1990 the company
teamed with Steven Spielberg to create syndicated cartoons for
television, and the reborn *Taz of Taz-Mania!* appeared the
following year with his own 65-episode series. Not only did TV
guarantee far greater exposure than film, Taz now had a genuine
fictional identity: eighteen years old, a cave home, parents, a
brother and sister, a job, a pet, a friend, a rival and an enemy.

A number of other factors lay behind the success. He
appealed equally to children, teenagers and adults, and on some
networks *Taz of Taz-Mania!* moved into adult time slots. He
rode the crest of a new merchandising wave through catalogue
shopping and the proliferation of Warner Bros. Studio Stores
across the United States and into Europe and Asia. He ranked
high in 'pop iconography . . . the rise of animation fandom'.[2]

Real Tasmanians were bound to take notice and 1997 marked the beginning of an interesting relationship between the entertainment giant and the Tasmanian state government. A front-page report in the *Sunday Tasmanian* newspaper, headlined 'We Lose Millions as Yanks Grab Devil', initiated proceedings:

> A multinational company makes millions of dollars out of the Tasmanian Devil—and Tassie does not get a cent. US company Warner Bros. owns the Tasmanian Devil. The international entertainment giant rakes in a fortune from its world-famous cartoon character Taz. The Devil ranks with Bugs Bunny and the Road Runner in the top three most popular characters worldwide—and its sales are increasing dramatically . . .
>
> Warner Bros. International public relations consumer products director Annie Morita said the Tasmanian Devil was one of the rising stars of its merchandising. 'I don't know if I could even attach a number,' she said. 'You'd have to think about everything from home videos, to music to television to studio stores to licensing. He's up there with all of that. You're talking millions if not billions.' She also noted that Taz was even bigger than Bugs in Brazil, Argentina, Mexico and Venezuela because 'they feel he represents the machismo of the region.'[3]

She was not exaggerating. A 1995 Warner Bros. survey had shown that about 95 per cent of US residents recognised Taz. Adult men liked his 'aggressive behaviour', teenagers 'identified with his rebellious streak', and children liked his generally wild manner.[4]

The report also noted a push to link Taz to the Sydney 2000 Olympic Games, as part of a campaign to promote Tasmania internationally. It would require a joint venture between the

Commonwealth government, Tourism Tasmania and Warner Bros., with Taz hosting a virtual tour of the island's tourist draw-cards such as its wilderness areas, wineries and Mount Wellington. For the backers of the concept, the cartoon devil 'attracted the sort of international attention money could not buy. Tasmania should cash in on Warner Bros.' investment'.[5]

Many Tasmanians knew of the cartoon character. Few, however, had any notion that their iconic marsupial could somehow be 'owned'. The report enlightened them:

> Warner Bros. has trademarked the character and registered the name Tasmanian Devil. The patent covers everything from sports gear, dolls, video games and Christmas decorations to underwear. And it is policed. Warner Bros.' Australian legal arm is tracking the source of illicit Tasmanian Devil dolls sold at the Royal Adelaide Show with a view to prosecution. One Tasmanian company, under threat of legal action, battled the international giant for eight years after being told not to use Tasmanian Devil as a brand name. Warner Bros. eventually gave the Tassie firm, Wigston's Lures, a one-off agreement allowing it to call a fishing lure a Tasmanian Devil.
>
> 'We're the only people other than Warner Bros. to have that registration and we fought tooth and nail to get the darn

The name 'Tasmanian Devil' is copyrighted to Warner Bros. Wigston's Lures, a small Hobart fishing lure company, spent eight years battling for the right to use the name Tasmanian Devil for one of its lures. Wigston's Tasmanian Devil *is a 13.5 gram 'Beetle Bomb'. (Courtesy Garth Wigston)*

thing,' Stuart Wigston said. 'It's hard to believe something indigenous to Tasmania is registered by a huge, great, multinational company. It's unreal . . .'[6]

The report went further, roping in Tasmania's internationally successful catamaran-building company Incat, which owner Bob Clifford had developed using unique aluminium wave-piercing hulls. It noted that:

Incat Tasmania steered clear of calling its new vessel the Tasmanian Devil—opting for '91-metre Devil'. A disclaimer circulated at the catamaran's launch . . . stated: 'No challenge to Warner Bros.' ownership is intended or implied[:] the devil livery on the 91-metre vessel bears no resemblance to the cartoon character.'[7]

Warner Bros. was asked to respond to the newspaper report. Its Australian lawyer stated that the company pursued offenders:

We've got a duty to go out there and police the marketplace so people don't abuse the system . . . If someone was to use Tasmanian Devil as a trademark we would regard that as an infringement of our registration but it really depends on [the] circumstances in which they used it. If someone was talking about the Tasmanian devil in Tasmania, that's a different situation . . . The trademark is not designed to stop the public from using the expression or to stop someone calling a Tasmanian devil a Tasmanian devil. It's more or less a brand name for goods.[8]

Needless to say the report created political waves. Tasmania's then Tourism Minister, Ray Groom, protested:

It seems so unfair [Groom told the *Sunday Tasmanian*]. Here we are, a small island below Australia with half a million people. We've got the devil as a native animal which doesn't exist anywhere else and a big American international company has pinched our rights . . . Warner Bros. are pretty tough operators, they know how to get their copyrights and their trademarks registered around the world where it counts. They endeavour to tie it all up . . . It could finish up in the courts and we'll be looking at that issue as well, to see what we can do to retrieve the rights to use our devil as we want to.[9]

Groom did concede that amicable negotiations were preferred, and to that end a Tasmanian delegation drew up preparations to visit Warner Bros. in Los Angeles for discussions.

Letter-writers to the newspaper didn't hold back. From Marcus Rowell, Hobart:

I have recently returned from a trip to South America where I was astonished to find that almost everybody knew the Warner Bros. Tasmanian Devil . . . certainly this character Taz is an identity that is internationally known who should be leading Tasmania's international marketing effort. Although we do need to make sure potential visitors know that he is fictitious as some South Americans expressed great concern that we have such a fierce creature in our wilderness.

From Craig Wellington, Hobart:

It seems to me Warner Bros. took the initiative long before anyone in Tasmania did and made the Tasmanian devil a household name around the world. They have obviously invested vast amounts in their characterisation of the Tasmanian devil and it is understandable that they wish to protect that investment by policing the use of their trademark character. It also seems to me their investment has given the devil a massive international profile. Tasmania should be grateful for such a gift. I know it's a cliché in the tourism industry to say 'Look what Crocodile Dundee did for the Northern Territory' but the Tasmanian devil provides us a similar, if not better, opportunity . . . have the Tasmanian devil declared a state emblem (rather than its extinct cousin) . . .

From John Williams, Glebe, Hobart:

The attitude of Tasmanian politicians that it is all right to rip-off Warner Bros.' trademarked figure, whatever their reasoning, is deplorable. It reinforces the low opinion which the public has of politicians' ethical standards. The reputation of the whole State must also suffer when prospective investors learn that we have such slippery standards in commercial dealings. And anyone who is trying to raise children with a respect for other people's property will be horrified at the example the politicians are setting. Warner Bros. have abided by the system our politicians have set up. I don't know if lawmakers are as careless in other countries. Would, for instance, an Australian company be able to register 'American bald eagle' in the United States of America?

From Barry Giles, Cambridge, Tasmania:

I recently returned to Tasmania . . . When we arrived in the US about five years ago there was already a vast amount of merchandise in the shops bearing the Tassie devil image . . . most Americans do not realise the animal or the island exist. Actually this is not surprising considering the results of surveys showing their appalling lack of knowledge about the geography of their own continent. You can hardly expect them to know about a distant 'fantasy' island on the other side of the planet. It's a standing joke that Tas . . . Taz . . . is in Africa.[10]

Lively political debate in the Tasmanian parliament followed the government delegation visit to Warner Bros. Groom was pressured to announce a good outcome:

Mr Polley: Can the minister inform the House of the outcome of the negotiations with Warner Bros. and when can we expect to see the internationally-recognised and popular cartoon character being used to promote Tasmania throughout the world?

Mr Groom: Constructive discussions took place and extremely interesting ideas were discussed. I might say contrary to some of the earlier indications the people from Warner Bros. were keen to embrace Tasmania . . . I will not go into the details at the moment because it will be a bit later on when we will discuss this in further detail and make some announcements, one would hope. But they are keen on the environmental aspects of Tasmania—how we can link Taz the Tazzie Devil into promoting internationally environmental issues focusing in part on Tasmania. The indications are this is not going to cost us the millions of dollars we thought . . . I have, Mr Speaker, so many Tazzie Devils coming out of my fax machine—not actual devils but different designs of devils from all sorts of people around Tasmania . . . Some very exciting ideas based upon our wonderful native animal, the Tasmanian devil, others not looking so happy, probably not the sort of thing we would want to use . . . We are looking at these, Mr Speaker, to see how we can use the Tasmanian Devil. It has a lot going for it . . . We are very pleased with the attitude shown by Warner Bros. They appreciate that we have produced this animal—they have used the animal for their own commercial benefits and my argument is that we should gain the benefit, we should be able to use this cartoon character based on our own animal widely around the world to promote Tasmania.[11]

Seven months later Groom announced that a verbal deal had been struck, in which the Tasmanian government would pay Warner Bros. an annual fee to use the Taz image for marketing purposes. Speculation on the cost ranged from a low of A\$50 000 to a high of ten times that amount, with all sorts of possibilities enthusiastically rumoured: Taz would feature in the opening ceremony of the Sydney 2000 Olympics; he would appear on Tasmanian tourist brochures in the United States, Canada, Europe and Asia; and a human in a Taz suit would become a feature of major world events such as the Berlin International Travel Show and the Melbourne Grand Prix.

In the 1990s the Tasmanian government lobbied Warner Bros. to allow use of the Taz image to promote Tasmania internationally. Warner Bros. declined. (Taz courtesy of Warner Bros. Taz, Tasmanian Devil and all related characters and elements are trademarks of and © Warner Bros. Entertainment Inc.)

Groom enthused particularly about the Games, declaring Taz to be integral to a Tasmanian push so significant that 'it's developing bigger than Ben Hur', though he did concede that 'whether we can get him on the main arena in the opening ceremony is a tough one'—suggesting a battle with the Games organisers—and furthermore, that the battle with Warner Bros. wasn't quite over either: 'No contracts are signed yet but we have understandings'.[12]

Whatever those understandings were, they dissolved, and the Games duly went ahead without Taz. But the issue was about more than the mere commercial opportunism represented by the cartoon figure, because its real counterpart represented an idealised opposite: a rare and elusive creature inhabiting an unspoilt wilderness.

During the parliamentary debates the Tasmanian Greens' Peg Putt had pointed this out. In 1997 debate raged over the conservative Federal Government's proposed Regional Forest Agreement (RFA)—would it protect or destroy Tasmania's old growth forests?—and Putt stated the obvious:

> Tourism is booming. Tourism is providing more and more jobs and tourism to Tasmania is promoted very much on the basis of 'Tasmania our natural State'. Our distinguishing feature in the international market is our wilderness and our beautiful places, our forests and our World Heritage areas, and if the RFA fails to protect that resource for the tourism industry then it will have failed. Only today we have had the announcement about Warner Bros. looking at promoting Tasmania with the Tasmanian devil focusing particularly on environmental protection. That is where a big-jobs future for our native forests lies.[13]

Warner Bros. appeared to have no particular history of championing distant environmental causes. Why should it stipulate that its cartoon character be linked to 'environmental issues focusing in part on Tasmania' (to quote Groom)? The Tasmanian Government–Warner Bros. verbal agreement, whatever it had been or not been, evaporated. Perhaps the environmental bar was set too high for the avidly pro-forestry government. Perhaps it wanted no bar at all.

11 DEVIL FACIAL TUMOUR DISEASE

All the visitors at Bronte Chalet leaned forward to see one of the world's most famous marsupials, the Tasmanian devil. His ears were pricked forward and there was almost a teddy-bear-like quality to his face as he moved towards his meal. Suddenly he turned and people reeled back in shock and horror. One whole side of his head was covered in a massive tumour like someone had stuck a slab of raw meat against his face. That was the last time we saw the devil nicknamed Phantom of the Opera alive . . . Mystical shocked me when her head first appeared as her face seemed to leap towards me. I then realised both lower jaws were covered in huge suppurating tumours. Amazingly her body condition was healthy with a big fat tail and she was even lactating and had young deposited in a nest somewhere. She was only three years old.

INGRID ALBION, LAUDERDALE

Christo Baars is a Dutch wildlife photographer whose portfolio includes striking images of Tasmanian devils. In

1996, near Mount William in the state's far northeast, he chanced to photograph a number of devils with ghastly facial growths. Back in Hobart Baars showed the photographs to Nick Mooney, who was horrified. Facial wounds, scars and abscesses are common in older devils, but Mooney recognised something quite different. Although cancer is a major cause of devil mortality, it's usually internal. In 20 years as a wildlife officer he had never seen such gross external manifestations.

The discovery coincided with anecdotal reports from farmers in the northeast of a drop in devil numbers. Dead sheep and cows lay uneaten in paddocks. Interestingly, this part of the state has always been associated with high concentrations of devils.

Cancer-like facial lumps and lesions were not entirely unknown. In 1984 at Mount William, David Pemberton trapped a devil with an apparent facial tumour, and there was an anecdotal report of a similar condition in the north of the state, in about 1993. After the Devil Facial Tumour Disease (DFTD) issue became public in late 2003, reports began to be received from a few old-timers of tumorous-looking devils back in the 1950s and 1960s in a variety of locations, from Ben Lomond in the east to Lake Pedder in the southwest and Arthur Plains in the northwest. But Eric Guiler, who saw and handled thousands of devils over 50 years throughout the island, never encountered it, and there is no evidence to back the old-timers' stories.

Others who worked extensively with devils in the 1970s and 1980s, without finding any trace of disease, included Bob Green (senior curator at the Queen Victoria Museum and Art Gallery) and Leon Hughes of the University of Queensland.

On the other hand, evidence for DFTD may be present in nineteenth-century devil skulls in collections in Berlin, Paris and London studied by Kathryn Medlock, zoology curator at the Tasmanian Museum and Art Gallery, while on a Churchill Fellowship in 2004. She observed deformities in some skulls similar to those seen in devils killed by DFTD.

A belief persists that devil populations have significant plague-and-crash phases, with numbers apparently much reduced in the 1860s, early 1900s and 1940s, with each recovery phase taking about 30 years. This requires examination of a possible recurrent disease as an explanation for the phenomenon.

The likelihood of DFTD being a naturally recurring virus—with, therefore, a 'natural' trigger—increases if distinct patterns of disease-induced population crashes are established. While there is anecdotal information suggesting periodic declines or crashes, hard evidence is scarce and contradictions are apparent.

In 1850 Louisa Anne Meredith recorded that devils were numerous where she lived on the east coast, 143 being caught by shepherds at Apsley in the course of one winter.[1] This is the only known historical reference to a significant catch-effort regime. There is no complementary data indicating low populations. Those devils were caught in pitfall traps dug for thylacines for bounty claims. They were also an efficient way to trap devils.

In 1863 John Gould wrote of the devil:

It has now become so scarce in all the cultivated districts, that it is rarely if ever seen there in a state of nature: there are yet, however, large districts in Van Diemen's Land untrodden by man; and such localities, particularly the rock gullies and vast forests on the western side of the island, afford it a secure retreat.[2]

Gould spent three months in Tasmania, travelling from Port Arthur in the south to George Town in the north, as well as to

Recherche Bay. He was an experienced bird and mammal collector, but if he personally saw few devils, which is likely, and used that as the basis of his report, the Meredith report should be judged more empirically sound. Eric Guiler believed that early twentieth-century reports of devil rarity largely repeated Gould's comment without further evaluation of numbers.

Professor Flynn struggled to find devils for research purposes and obtained just one female in 1911. He had not necessarily tried too hard, however, he asked a resident of the northern Hobart suburb of Bridgewater to get him one. It took a few weeks, suggesting scarcity in the Bridgewater area! A year earlier *The Mercury* had reported that 'one would have to go a long way from Hobart now to find a Tasmanian devil, as they are even scarcer than the "tiger"'.[3]

Thylacines were hunted and killed in large numbers over many years and Guiler has compiled accurate bounty records showing consistent annual returns. It is hard data. Yet his own belief of a major disease-induced crash early in the twentieth century may be based on flimsy evidence. He wrote: 'Several men have stated to me that decline was very rapid and occurred almost simultaneously throughout Tasmania and one grazier stated that all the Dasyures disappeared about 1910, claiming that a disease like distemper killed them'.[4] These claims aren't much to go on, but the published paper in which they appeared was subsequently quoted extensively, and there is no other known written record to strengthen the claims.

Clive Lord of the Tasmanian Museum and Art Gallery wrote in 1918 that 'it [the devil] is now only met with in the rugged unsettled districts';[5] a few years later, he more optimistically stated that 'in the rougher sections of the country this species exists in fair numbers and there is every prospect of it remaining an inhabitant of such places for years to come'.[6]

The suggestion of scarcity where humans lived doesn't imply depressed populations throughout Tasmania, although the words of Gould, Flynn and others were widely accepted. However, in 1924, Herbert Hedley Scott, longtime director of the Queen Victoria Museum, and Clive Lord wrote:

> We are aware that certain Zoologists are of the opinion that the species is in danger of extinction, and we will readily admit that it is difficult to secure perfect specimens when required, but that is readily explained by the class of country which the species now occupies.[7]

Their case was that devils were not rare but difficult to catch without significant effort. It could not have been easy before the advent of lightweight traps, four-wheel drives and extensive road systems. Nonetheless, Guiler later maintained that devils were rare at that time.

In 1946, while searching for thylacines, David Fleay caught nineteen devils in the Jane River area of the west coast. This suggests plenty. Guiler's response was that extensive use of attractive baits might have been expected to have yielded even more, which would have been a true indicator of abundance. (Suggesting rarity, however, it is true that a devil caught on a farm in the 1940s was sent to Launceston's Queen Victoria Museum and Art Gallery for identification. Equally true is that in 2003 a barred bandicoot was presented to the Tasmanian Museum and Art Gallery as a baby thylacine.)

During the 1960s and 1970s applications for permits to cull devils increased, along with numerous reports to the Parks and Wildlife Service of apparent, though not quantitatively confirmed, increases in devil numbers.

From all of the above it may reasonably be inferred that the devil population is difficult to calculate without systematic trapping. An area seemingly empty of devils may have them in good numbers. Radio tracking studies have revealed devils foraging within 50 metres of a barbecue without having been detected. Devils with radio collars have been tracked to their resting sites under grass sags where they have never been previously detected. Devils denned in thick fern patches can be unsighted from a few paces. Devils tracked at night have walked around the researcher at a distance of less than 3 metres without being seen. David Pemberton's three years of fieldwork, involving many months in an area where over 200 devils lived, yielded only a dozen sightings when on foot.

In the light of this, earlier reports of devil population fluctuations need to be treated with care, as should the notion that a distemper-like or mange-like disease affected dasyures early in the twentieth century. When Professor Flynn was researching devils, at a time when they were supposedly scarce, he wrote of his official duty to research marsupial diseases. In his 'Report of Ralston Professor of Biology for the Year ending June 30th 1919', he recorded that, 'it is only occasionally that such diseases are brought to me personally'.[8]

Persecution of the thylacine and the devil reduced their numbers. In the mid-1880s Melbourne author and journalist Howard Willoughby wrote of the devil and tiger that 'both have been so hunted and trapped by the settlers, whose sheep and poultry they killed, as now to be very scarce'.[9]

Some reports indicated that by the turn of the twentieth

century devils were so abundant that they were heavily persecuted. According to Lewis Stevenson, an old-timer who in 1972
was interviewed by environmental activist Bob Brown:

> In 1900 there were more devils than rabbits. We caught as
> many as eight in a pitfall at night. They were trapped and
> snared and poisoned and got the mange like the tigers, so did
> wombats. From 1906 onwards they died out. 1914, the
> drought year, was the worst year for the mange. All their hair
> fell out and left the black skins bare in the bad ones. Their eyes
> and eye sight was not affected but it sent badgers [wombats]
> totally blind.[10]

The pitfall trap was part of an elaborate trapping system for
thylacines. The thylacine bounty provided financial incentive
for snarers to increase their efforts, and the devil by-catch was
undoubtedly significant. According to *The Mercury* in 1910:
'The "devil" is a slow, clumsy animal, without the speed or

Persecution of devils continues, despite the threat to them from DFTD. The remains of these persecuted devils were found in a bag by the side of a road in 2004. (Courtesy Nick Mooney)

cunning of the "tiger" and is much more easily trapped . . .
[it] will walk open-eyed into any trap which contains a bit
of strong-smelling meat.'[11] This may only point to the Tasmanian devil not caring for urban environments and being more
common in the bush. The ease of capture supports the
contention of probably high human-induced mortality rates of
devils during that era of intense thylacine trapping.

Tasmanian devils may well have undergone a decline early in
the 1900s, but there is no hard evidence disease was the cause.
What is certain is that persecution of the animal by a variety of
means, together with land clearing, affected the population
through unnatural reduction in numbers and population dis-
placement and fragmentation. Any high-density population
today that suffered mortalities of eight animals a night, as
reported by Stevenson, would be wiped out in a few years.

In 1999 Menna Jones, researching devils along Tasmania's
east coast, observed some with tumours near Little Swanport,
more than 250 kilometres south of where Baars had taken his
photographs in 1996. Two years later she trapped three
tumorous devils on the Freycinet Peninsula. Her subsequent
monitoring there indicated that the peninsula's population was
in serious decline.

Nick Mooney's trapping made him painfully aware of how
the disease was spreading. In March 2003 he wrote an internal
Parks and Wildlife departmental memo calling for more assistance to combat the problem. That meant funding. The memo's
advice and recommendations were not acted on, despite government knowledge of the seriousness of the issue: in answer to a
question in Parliament on 20 August 2003, Environment
Minister Bryan Green stated that in some areas devil populations

had crashed by 85 per cent. Instead of funding, for baseline studies in particular, an essentially cost-free working group was formed, comprising veterinarians, wildlife specialists and veterinary pathologists.

Mooney went public. On 1 September 2003, the front-page headline in *The Mercury* read, 'Tassie Devil Under Threat'. The report, and a detailed feature on the problem, meant that for the first time the public became aware of the bizarre DFTD and its potentially disastrous consequence of extinction. Among the disturbing revelations: that virtually nothing was known about the disease, its origins, or whether or how it was transferred from animal to animal; that it spread through the body, and dissolved skull bone; that Tasmania's government animal health laboratory, at Mount Pleasant in Launceston, had neither the expertise nor staff to investigate it; that quarantining devils on islands (or repopulating the mainland) carried risks because even healthy-looking devils might be carriers; that devils might now be fatally susceptible to an emerging fox population; that research could take three years or more to establish the genetic sequence of a virus, should the disease be caused by a virus; that environmental pollutants might be involved; and that the disease might be capable of crossing to other species such as quolls.

One positive, if it could be called that, lay in the slow travelling speed of DFTD through areas of dispersed devil populations. In those areas the natural breeding patterns might be sufficient to match the disease.

Wildlife park owner Androo Kelly noted that low devil numbers left them more vulnerable than ever to persecution through poisoning, trapping and shooting, and he also took issue with political insensitivity to wildlife:

> There's a new culture in the top level of government. Wildlife is just tucked in with primary industries and the agenda is primary-industry driven. We don't do enough about wildlife disease. People outside this State can't believe that we don't have a response to something affecting such an icon animal in our environment . . . We don't give them enough respect.[12]

How best, then, to tackle the mystery disease? The scientific starting point for DFTD assumed that it could be a retrovirus, that is, a virus occurring naturally in devil DNA but lying dormant until triggered, at which point it attacks cell DNA. Small lumps or lesions first appear in and around the mouth, which grow rapidly into tumours. Death through breakdown of body functions and starvation usually occurs within five months.[13]

The analysis is essentially a two-step process. Identifying the type of cancer cells involved is the first step, but is a complex one, since it involves analysing cancerous cells which have changed dramatically from when they were healthy. Equally important is identifying from what part of the body they originated, such as from muscles, lymph or skin. Once the type of cancer has been determined, the second step is to identify the possible causes of the disease, namely the trigger or triggers. Speculation as to those would ensure that Tasmania's newest environmental problem would not be confined to laboratory microscopes.

In fact, the next day a revelation about the Mooney Parks and Wildlife memo intensified focus on the political response to the crisis, as two versions of Mooney's document came to light. In the original, written as a brief to inform Environment Minister Green of the situation, Mooney had written that funding for baseline monitoring of devils had been 'recommended on many occasions but never resourced',[14] and that new funds were needed to investigate the disease. The Tasmanian Greens party made this document public. The second, altered version—the 'official' memo which landed on Green's desk—omitted this critical phrase (critical in both senses of the word), and also said that the situation would be dealt with within the current budget.

Ironically, back in 1987 monitoring studies had been recommended for the Mount William area—precisely where, nine years later, Baars was to provide graphic evidence of the disease.

At this point, with a few thousand dollars shifted from other projects, Mooney and a visiting US colleague, Marco Restani, embarked on a statewide snapshot survey, which was to prove of critical importance. Forty sites were chosen across the state, excepting the southwest, and

> . . . each of these 40 sites was sampled for one night with 30 traps spread strategically (set in the sorts of places devils were likely to be caught) along 10 km of road . . . Devils were caught at 23 of 40 sites, five sites of which showed DFTD-affected individuals. At six other sites, an apparent 'footprint' of DFTD was detected (multiple juveniles only or no devils in areas where they were recently very common and multiple captures could be expected). DFTD appeared to be spread over much of the eastern half of Tasmania.[15]

A *Mercury* editorial, meanwhile, took to task the political sanitising of Mooney's memo:

> Tasmania has two types of feisty devils. One wears a green Guernsey and is thriving in the VFL [Victorian Football League]. The other is facing a threat that could drive it to the edge of extinction. This hideous possibility, given the infamy

that the thylacine's death has earned Tasmania, should be thoroughly exercising the minds of Premier Jim Bacon and Environment Minister Bryan Green. They should contemplate that, despite what the history books might record about their achievements, presiding over the demise of the animal that has come to symbolise Tasmania around the world would earn them a special place . . . The Government should be responding on several levels to the disease, and keeping Tasmanians fully informed along the way. It needs a strategy, as Mr Mooney suggests, to ensure the survival of the species. The thylacine's extinction, so most believe, is an inglorious event in our history. It is a reminder of our environmental insensitivity and inability to act to conserve a threatened species. It must not happen again.[16]

Bacon soon afterwards announced, in his first statement on the disease, that research into the virus would be 'fast-tracked'. On the same day David Parer entered the debate. In 30 years of making wildlife documentaries around the world he had seen enough evidence of species decline and extinction to fear that a pattern of sustained habitat destruction may have triggered the disease.

Veterinary pathologist Dr David Obendorf sounded another warning, commenting that lack of knowledge of and control over endemic diseases in wild animals could have adverse implications for Tasmania's status as a disease-free island, should the devil disease ever be transmitted to livestock. Understanding livestock diseases meant little without equal understanding of their equivalents in wildlife, and he cited as an example the role of wallabies in the spread of the sheep-wasting disease OJD.

Obendorf, Parer and Mooney weren't alone with their frustrations and fears. Restani speculated that:

carnivores, such as the devil, often reflect ecosystem health . . .
In my opinion, the disease epizootic signals us to take note of
the current condition of Tasmanian ecosystems, particularly
the interactions among devils, feral cats, quolls and foxes . . .
As a scientist with 20 years' experience studying wildlife
throughout the US, Canada and Greenland, I have seen only
sylvatic plague rival the population destruction wrought by
the devil disease. We know nothing . . . and are helpless to
develop an effective conservation strategy.[17]

Numerous potential triggers were suggested: the rabbit-
killing calicivirus; the widespread use of 1080 poison; farm
chemicals, especially organophosphates; and land clearance. In
an island with as much bush and large tracts of remote wilderness as Tasmania, land clearance seems an unlikely cause of a
virulent disease, but resulting population fragmentation might
be a cause: when populations become physically cut off from one
another they inbreed, and the resulting lack of genetic diversity,
already low in an island population, might trigger the action of a
dormant retrovirus. Isolated populations can also become
stressed if overcrowding occurs. Stressed animals are invariably
more susceptible to disease.

While it may be plausible to contemplate a natural virus
keeping control over population explosions, it's equally the case
that with each successive crash the genetic diversity of the
species changes and probably diminishes. The implication of
this, if it is correct, is that the devil is on a self-inflicted trajec-
tory to extinction. (Dingoes and humans are assumed to have
wiped out mainland devils. But could devils there have experienced natural population crashes from which they eventually
couldn't recover, through population fragmentation across the

vast continent into pools of very low genetic diversification?)

At the other end of the spectrum, the devil may have become the victim of the virus 'crossing over' from another species. Mount Pleasant pathologist Roy Mason, familiar with viral tumours affecting cats, speculated that feral cats may have transferred the virus to devils through fighting. Adult male cats are most susceptible to tumours, from fighting one another, and adult male devils, which accumulate many bite scars, have the highest rate of DFTD.

A number of retroviral sequences have jumped species barriers, including HIV/AIDS and SARS. And occasionally a cocktail of factors come into play. In South-East Asia land clearing destroyed the natural habitat of a bat species, and the bats began to roost in trees above pig pens. Their faeces, urine and dead bodies dropped into the pens and were ingested by the pigs. The pigs' owners and their families contracted the bat virus. Efforts to rid Melbourne's botanic gardens of fruit bats have resulted in some migrating to King Island in Bass Strait. Seals there could ingest dead bats. Those seals that are attracted to fish farms in the region are relocated to other Tasmanian waters (about 700 a year), potentially, therefore, transmitting a virus from another species to a distant location. It's an unlikely way of an exotic disease infiltrating a seemingly secure island—but only as unlikely as the possibility ten years ago that devils were about to face an extinction crisis.

Control of wild animals for economic reasons is hardly unique to Tasmania but it is the manner in which it is done that can prove contentious, especially if it threatens Tasmania's remaining carnivorous marsupial icon. Rabbit calicivirus has been cited as a potential cause of or contributor to the disease.

Calicivirus was introduced in 1996 in the latest effort to control rabbits. Devils, of course, eat dead rabbits . . .

Devils also eat dead wallabies, kangaroos, pademelons and possums, which are targeted by the forestry industry because they eat tree seedlings. Once an area has been selected for plantation forestry, whether through clear-felling or conversion of farmland, and seeds sewn aerially or manually, the area is then scattered with carrots laced with the chemical toxin sodium monofluoroacetate (1080 poison). The result is good for seedlings but devastating to the browsers. The kill estimate of Forestry Tasmania and private plantation owners for the year 2003 was just under 100 000 macropods. As well as devils, endangered quolls and wedge-tailed eagles eat these poisoned carcasses, and domestic dogs are known to have died this way. The continued use of 1080 has caused much public anger in Tasmania. At the least, mass kills of browsers impacts locally upon devil populations, where suddenly their main prey base disappears.

Nick Mooney, while not discounting 1080, considers agricultural pesticides and forestry plantation sprays to have more obviously lethal potential to trigger the disease, given that some have carcinogenic properties—as does diesel fuel, which is used in vast quantities in rural Tasmania, and there is no doubt devils come into contact with it.

If any of these primary industry products, or a combination of them, were found to be the trigger, the management consequences would be profound.

There is always more. Over decades in the twentieth century, Australia, the United States and other countries solved a rural problem of dusty roads by regularly spraying them with an oil-based, liquid industrial waste. This liquid was laced with manmade toxic chemicals, PCBs (polychlorinated biphenyls), used in the manufacture of products including coolants, hydraulic fluids, paints, newsprint and varnishes. Some of the toxins have a life of hundreds of years, and many roads in the United States have been dug up in detoxification programs. PCBs were used in Tasmania until 1987, a decade after being banned in the United States and Europe, because they 'cause cancer and many other problems in animals', and in humans they 'may damage the immune system, hinder sexual development and impair intellectual ability'.[18]

Official recognition of the potential role of toxins as triggers for DFTD followed:

> A pilot trial is proposed in which statistically valid numbers of tissue samples from affected and unaffected devils will be selected and tested for the presence of a range of toxins. It is proposed that the 10 most commonly isolated toxins are then exposed to normal devil cell cultures in amounts similar to those found in affected devils and any changes in the cells noted. If there are positive effects of the toxins on the cell cultures then there is an indication that a much larger project is warranted and should be undertaken.[19]

From a peak of an estimated 150 000 devils in the mid-1990s, the state's numbers had dropped by at least a third. Menna Jones concluded that a reduction to 15 000 could make extinction in the wild irreversible. The call grew to isolate healthy devils on an offshore island. But that carried its own set of potential problems. Against this backdrop, the first major step in tackling the disease came with the arrangement of a specialists' workshop, held in Launceston on 14 October 2003. It was not before time.

The workshop got off to a controversial start. Despite widespread interest, the public was admitted only to the opening address by Environment Minister Green. Some participating scientists expressed surprise, wondering if the ban was intended to minimise potential negative political fallout. On the other hand, experts in deep discussion on a dilemma they knew little about could probably do without public attention, although interested scientists were also kept out and others had to indulge in manipulation to be invited. A media brief had to suffice for the public. It noted the key role of the devil in the state's ecology and that all sections of the community had a role to play. In a practical sense, this might mean notifying authorities of, say, a diseased roadkill devil; it was also surely a plea to those rural Tasmanians for whom devil-killing remained a sport or duty.

Some 55 invited specialists, local and interstate, attended the workshop. It was a high-powered and unique gathering. As an icon species the Tasmanian devil ranks with endangered wildlife such as the panda, Asian tiger and American bald eagle, yet the apparent suddenness of its extinction threat created an added urgency. Introductory presentations were followed by a koala leukemia case study. A plenary session identified key issues, and afternoon sessions were devoted to pathology and epidemiology, population monitoring and mapping and management responses.

A paper on options for management included data on the potential for establishing populations on one or more of Tasmania's offshore islands. Selection criteria included size, a preference for public land, diverse habitat and suitable prey species, accessibility for monitoring, and an absence of vulnerable ground-nesting birds and small mammals. In Menna Jones' estimate, a minimum of 40 devils would be required to represent full genetic diversity, with a minimum of 3 square kilometres per animal, which ruled out many of the smaller islands. (Tasmania has 334 offshore islands.)

Quarantining healthy devils in this way may appear straight-forward, but a range of complications arises in relocation, including lack of genetic diversity, potential failure of the animals to establish themselves, impacts on existing wildlife, management of the predator–prey ratio, and the fact that such a relocation could be irreversible and damage equally important conservation attributes of the islands.

A flowchart presented at the workshop indicated just how complicated the issue had become. This is reproduced on page 188.

Case by case disease studies were presented at the workshop in order to lead to a better understanding of devil cancers, as the first step in arriving at a clinical definition of DFTD, including this first 'official' case from 1995:

History—A female Tasmanian Devil of unknown age was found at Greens Beach. Gross—very poor skin condition—hairless over much of surface, scabby, morocco leather-like patches, especially in the groin and flank. Subcutaneous lymph nodes enlarged and also scattered dermal and subcutaneous swellings. Necrotic reactionary lesion in the masseter muscle. The internal visceral organs appeared normal. Masses of cestodes (tapeworms) in the jejunum and moderate numbers in the ileum, plus there were ascarid-like nematodes mainly in the duodenal area. Histology— multifocal dermal leukosis with lymphosarcomatous infiltration of lymph nodes and in the periportal tissues of the liver and

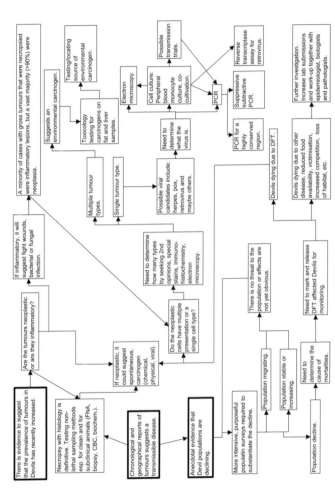

The first gathering of specialists to combat DFTD took place in Launceston in October 2003. This flowchart gives some idea of the complexities of the issue facing the 55 biologists, veterinary pathologists, marsupial carnivore experts and others who attended the workshop. (Courtesy Department of Primary Industries, Water and Environment)

interstitially in the adrenal and also through skeletal muscle
tissue. The lesion in the masseter muscle was due to heavy
lymphosarcomatous infiltration of that muscle mass. This animal
was affected by widespread lymphosarcomatous neoplasia.
Diagnosis—Lymphosarcoma. Comment—There were occasional,
but consistent findings of azurophilic intracytoplasmic material
in some cells. Artefact or viral inclusions?[20]

Among the more disturbing findings to come out of the
workshop were that the disease might not be diagnosed for
another ten years, and that feral cats may already be rapidly filling
the emptied devil niche. The very next day Burnie police retrieved
a freshly dead fox from the Bass Highway near the seaside town's
old hospital. It might have been placed there as part of the obnox-
ious game being played by those importing foxes into the state,
but it was a reminder that not only cats might be a threat.

Another depressing outcome of the workshop, revealed
through release of internal Department of Primary Industries,
Water and Environment (DPIWE) documents, under freedom of
information legislation, appeared to confirm that government
reaction had been too slow, too late and too modest, with the
result that 'a happy ending to this issue' appeared 'very
unlikely'.[21] The consequences of a lack of long-term systematic
monitoring of such an important animal were obvious.

The comments were seized open by the two opposition political parties as damning evidence in the wake of the altered
Mooney memo. In parliament the Leader of the Opposition,
Rene Hidding, accused Premier Jim Bacon of being caught flat-
footed on the issue. Bacon hotly denied the charge. Later in the
day, Bryan Green, the Labor Party Environment Minister, and
Nick McKim, the Greens' Environment Spokesman, clashed:

Mr Green—. . . So it was I who generated the interest in the devils, it was I who generated all of the work that has been done since that time [the memo] on Tasmanian devils. Everything else that had been done had never formally come to the Government in any way, and that is the point. And this is the point that you ought to understand, and not smugly smile over there and kick back as if you are the great expert.

Mr McKim—I'm allowed to smile. Don't put words into my mouth; I've never claimed to be an expert on this. In fact I've said quite frankly that none of us is . . .

Mr Green—Mr Deputy Speaker, what I can say is that the State Government is extremely serious about this issue. I do not think we could be any more definite about an issue that has confronted us, any more serious about making sure that we do everything we possibly can to protect the devil. It is true it is an icon, it is true we do not understand what the disease is, but it is also true that we are doing what we have to do to make sure that we are given the best opportunity to understand the disease. We have done that in a number of ways, but I think I should keep this in perspective.

When we received the first briefs on this, it was about lesions; it was not talking about a disease as such, it was just talking about lesions. It was not until later on that people started talking about this in the context of a disease—

Mr Booth [Green]—Did you think they were marshmallows stuck on their face?

Mr Deputy Speaker—Order. If you want to speak, please speak from your own seat.

Mr Green—This is where these blokes really do stray outside the realm of decency when they talk about this—

Mr McKim—What would a lesion be if it wasn't a disease?[22]

The vexed question of funding stayed at the forefront of the issue. An earlier state government application for federal funding through the Wildlife and Exotic Diseases Preparedness Program—resulting in just $7000, which is all the program had left in its budget—obliged Green to again defend his position. A week later, Jim Bacon announced that the government would make $1.8 million available, over four years, to combat the disease, a 450-fold increase over the existing $40 000.

Warner Bros., with its long association with animal stars, had a record of backing causes to protect vulnerable wildlife in the United States. Thus in 1999 it had teamed with the US Fish and Wildlife Service and the City of New Orleans to create an Urban Treaty for Bird Conservation. This pilot program aimed to educate city dwellers in the importance of conserving migratory songbird populations, for many of which urban habitats are crucial. Tweety the canary was named Official Spokesbird.[23]

Warner Bros. had in fact been approached for help soon after the realisation that the disease was rampant, but its chief corporate communications officer, Barbara Brogliatti, had then firmly stated that, whatever else the company might contemplate, the use of the Taz image remained off limits. Now, however, came the newspaper scoop—with a feisty Taz superimposed over a pair of real devils, a rare legal commercial image—declaring:

> Warner Bros. is in advanced talks with the State Government over a rescue package for Tasmania's virus-riddled devil population. The US-based entertainment giant . . . is planning to join the effort to help save the Tasmanian Devil . . . It is understood negotiations have reached an advanced but delicate stage and an announcement with more detail is expected . . . spokeswoman Barbara Brogliatti told international news

agency Reuters last week: 'We are in discussions with the folks in Tasmania to see what we might be able to do to help . . . Firstly, as human beings [concerned about] any endangered species and, secondly, it is our beloved Taz'.[24]

These discussions with Tourism Tasmania moved forward to a point where, by the end of the year, Warner Bros. designers had come up with a pair of prototypes for Taz soft toys, wearing caps and t-shirts bearing save-the-devil slogans.

Funding issues aside, areas of progress became apparent. Scientists concluded the disease appeared to result in a single type of tumour, a possible step forward in the task of identifying its cause. And the Nature Conservation Branch put in place a long-term monitoring program for devil populations. In addition to regular trapping, monitoring techniques now included microchipping to replace ear tattooing, and the use in remote locations of automatically-triggered cameras set up at feeding sites. Early tests returned high-quality photographs of diseased animals.

Mooney's team in the field used a portable surgery that allowed biopsies and the removal of small early cancers. The team liased regularly with veterinarians from the state's Animal Health Laboratories, and also passed its results to the government-funded Devil Disease Task Force, which itself had linked with the CSIRO, Taronga Zoo in Sydney and Murdoch University in Western Australia. The task force included a range of specialist wildlife experts.

Working in the field had its own difficulties. To begin with, handling grossly disfigured animals required an ability to cope with repeated exposure to suffering, a reality made tougher by the decision not to euthanase except in the most extreme cases, where an animal was on the verge of death. Diseased animals

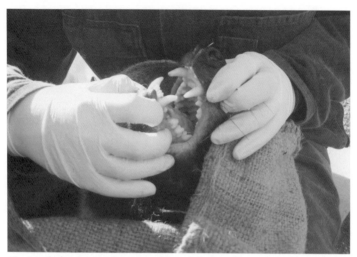

Many professionals and volunteers work in task forces combating the deadly disease.
(Courtesy Nick Mooney)

released with radio tracking collars provided valuable monitoring information. Others were lactating, with young denned somewhere. Set against this, fieldworkers had also to attempt to operate within the bounds of the *Animal Welfare Act*; a difficult balance to achieve, not least because the wording of the Act is very generalised.

A January 2004 survey at Table Mountain near Bothwell in the central highlands, undertaken by David Pemberton, showed a population crash of between 30 and 50 per cent. Traps were set at three locations over two nights in consistently pouring rain, which flooded creeks and paddocks and made the task difficult. Nonetheless seven devils were trapped. Two had DFTD, a third had cloacal ulcers. Pemberton's field notes of a moderately diseased female, which had pouch young, read:

The presence of disease on this animal was not obvious at first. I noticed slight red swelling on both lips, a slight swelling on the left muzzle and pus on one swollen follicle. Inspection of the mouth revealed two lesions, one on the upper palate measuring roughly 3 cm across and one on the lower measuring 2 cm across. Both lesions were maroon-red. The red swelling on the lips corresponded with swellings on the inside of the lips, which were pale yellow and red. The distinctive markings of this animal mean I could probably identify if we follow progression of the disease.[26]

Fieldwork hygiene took on a new significance. Gone were the days of clunky old metal box-traps and casual handling without gloves. Newly designed PVC tube-traps had to be disinfected after each use, as well as the sacks into which devils were placed so they could be measured and inspected. Unwittingly spreading the disease through efforts to combat it would be devastating, and for this reason it was decided to dispose of sacks after one use.

Chapter 3 sets out the many and varied relationships devils have with other creatures in the wild. And although Hobart Town surveyor G. P. Harris had them eating whale blubber in 1806, even he would surely have struggled to further the marine link by associating the devil with the humble oyster. But it came about. St Helens in northeast Tasmania is the largest town on the east coast, situated on Georges Bay, in which commercial oyster farming began in 1980. Between 1997 and 2003, incidents of high mortality and shell deformity seemed to follow heavy rain. Oyster farmers contracted Sydney-based marine ecologist Dr Marcus Scammell to investigate. He concluded that rainfall introduced a damaging causal agent into the bay, and subsequent wind-drift patterns in the intertidal zone, the area where the tides rise and fall within an estuary, floated that agent into the oyster farms.

Scammell's tests revealed the agent to be tri-butyl tin, a chemical long used in marine anti-fouling paint to keep boat hulls free of growths. Although banned from use in the paint, the chemical itself was still commercially available. Scammell's finding led to it being banned altogether. He concluded that other unknown agents might also be responsible.

In January 2004 following flood rains (the same rains affecting the Pemberton Table Mountain survey), Georges Bay experienced up to 90 per cent oyster mortality. Other filter feeders—mussels and barnacles—as well as prawns, crabs, sea urchins and even non-marine frogs and insects, died in large numbers. This time Scammell's investigations led him to focus on extensive forestry aerial spraying by helicopters the previous month. One of the helicopters had crashed. Tests of biocide spills at the crash site identified alpha-cypermethrin, atrazine, simazine, chlorothalonil and terbacil. They're as toxic as they sound, and Scammell noted:

> The importance of this information is not that it tells us what is at a small contaminated site, rather it tells us what is being sprayed over the vast area that these plantations cover . . . The normal environmental protection methods do not appear to be in place and no policing of the State's own Forestry Code of Practice appears to be occurring. More disturbingly, the problems associated with oysters also correlate with tumours and mortality in Tasmanian Devils. Further there appears to be a risk to human health as contamination of local drinking water supplies is also possible.[27]

Specially designed PVC tube traps reduce the risk of captured devils damaging themselves and can be efficiently disinfected after each use. (Courtesy Nick Mooney)

As soon as the devil and human connection was made, the story blossomed. In the wake of their $1.6 million loss, oyster farmers demanded that spraying cease until it could be proved that the biocides weren't to blame. The forestry industry reacted with anger. DFTD project manager Alistair Scott released a cautious statement saying that no clinical evidence linked the spraying to the devil disease. Environmental health expert Dr Mark Donohoe queried why atrazine, banned in most countries for its known ability to damage DNA and cause tumours in laboratory mice, was still commonly used in Tasmania.

At this time too, the separate but related Fox Taskforce steering committee began to fracture over its decision to issue 1080 poison to farmers to bury baits on their properties. The

Tasmanian Conservation Trust pulled out of the committee on two grounds: farmers were not specialised bait layers; and they were being used to cover up budget restraints.

Thus the politics of environmental management, a running sore for almost the life of the state, once again threatened to overwhelm the real business at hand: saving the Tasmanian devil.

Finally, the saga of the disease included a strange and poignant coincidence in the death of Jim Bacon, the premier of Tasmania since 1998, who succumbed to cancer in June 2004. Bacon was a man who could take a joke. In 2001, at a lavish function at Hobart's Cascade Brewery, which uses the thylacine on its labels, he launched *The Tragedy and Myth of the Tasmanian Tiger*, a CD-ROM created by filmmaker Steve Thomas. The making of it had necessarily required Thomas to work closely with staff of the Tasmanian Museum and Art Gallery, which holds the world's largest collection of thylacine material and data. David Pemberton, as zoology curator at the Museum, presented Bacon with a wrapped gift after he had made his launch speech. The hundred or so guests watched as Bacon unwrapped a large framed photograph. Digitally manipulated, it was a fresh roadkill scene: a four-wheel-drive vehicle with a Tasmanian government licence plate and a dead thylacine.

Bacon laughed, but the message clearly struck home. Two years later, on 2 September 2003, he spoke at a ceremony remembering the loss of the thylacine. A day earlier, Nick Mooney had gone public over the drastic state of the devil disease and the lack of government help to combat it. Ironically, therefore, Bacon found himself at a thylacine remembrance function saying, 'My government will not allow the Tasmanian devil to become extinct. That would be a tragedy. The devils are not going the same way as the thylacine did. That is too horrible a thought to contemplate.'[28]

After his speech Bacon conferred with Pemberton and then Mooney. He wanted confirmation that the extinction threat was real. They assured him it was. He then asked what funds were required, and was told of a program already budgeted for but not yet funded. Exactly one month later the existing $40 000 of government funding became the $1.8 million package.

The Tasmanian devil is a highly profitable, lucrative animal, an iconic wild species. It may recover without human assistance, but it is to be hoped and expected, that no effort will be spared in saving the world's largest marsupial carnivore.

NOTES

Chapter 1

1 Letter of Morton Allport to Curzon Allport, March 1863. Allport Library & Museum of Fine Arts.

2 Definitive studies were carried out by Lars Werdelin and documented in his 'Some Observations on *Sarcophilus laniarius* and the evolution of *Sarcophilus*', Records of the Queen Victoria Museum, vol. 90, 1987.

3 Scott, Alan, pers. comm., 1 July 2004.

4 ibid.

5 Guiler, Eric, *The Tasmanian Devil*, Hobart, St David's Park Publishing, 1992, p. 10.

6 *The Mercury*, 2 September 2003, p. 2.

7 Nowak, Ronald M., *Walker's Mammals of the World*, Baltimore, Johns Hopkins University Press, 1999, p. 64.

8 Nick Mooney email to David Pemberton, 8 November 2004.

9 Wilkie, A. A. W., as told to Osborn, A. R., 'Tasmanian Devils[:] Three Interesting Imps', in *Reminiscences From the Melbourne Zoo*, Melbourne, Whitcombe & Tombs, 1917, pp. 58–9.

10 Taylor, James, comp., *Zoo{:} Studies From Nature*, Sydney, James Taylor, 1920, p. 107.

11 Lord, Clive, 'Notes on the Mammals of Tasmania', in *Royal Society of Tasmania{:} Papers and Proceedings, 1918*, Hobart, The Society, 1918, p. 45.

12 Lord, Clive, 'Existing Tasmanian Marsupials', in *Royal Society of Tasmania{:} Papers and Proceedings, 1927*, Hobart, The Society, 1927, p. 22.

13 The publication was *The Children's Newspaper* and the story was reported in *The Mercury*, 17 February 1962, p. 9.

14 Farrand, John Jr. (ed.), *The Audubon Society Encyclopedia of Animal Life*, New York, Chanticleer Press, 1987 [Sixth Printing, 1988], p. 27. There is no author credit.

15 www.jonahcohen.com/jersey_devil. This website and many others are devoted to information about the State of New Jersey and its famous devil.

16 Lord, Clive, *A Synopsis of the Vertebrate Animals of Tasmania*, London, Oldham, Beddome & Meredith, 1924, p. [ii].

17 Cameron, Max, pers. comm., June 2004.

18 Fleay, David, 'The Tasmanian or Marsupial Devil—Its Habits and Family Life', *The Australian Museum Magazine*, vol. X, no. 9, 15 March 1952, p. 277–8.

19 Linnean Society of London, *Transactions*, vol. 9, 1808. 'Description of two new Species of Didelphis from Van Diemen's Land. By G. P. Harris, Esq. Communicated by the Right Honourable Sir Joseph Banks, Bart. K. B. Pres. R. S., H. M. L. S. Read April 21, 1807', reproduced in *Letters of GP Harris 1803–1812*, edited by Barbara Hamilton-Arnold, London, Arden Press, 1994, p. 90.

20 Fleay, David, op. cit., p. 279.

21 Wilkie, A. A. W., op. cit., pp. 58–9.

22 Grzimek, Bernhard, *Australians{:} Adventures with Animals and Men in Australia*, translated by J. Maxwell Brownjohn, London and Sydney, Collins, 1967, p. 278.

23 Fleay, op. cit., p. 278.

24 Guiler, op. cit., p. 18.

25 www.dpiwe.tas.gov.au/inter.nsf, p.7, accessed 30 December 2003.

26 Grey, Lionel, pers. comm., 10 July 2004.

27   ABC Radio, *PM*, 2 December 2002. www.abc.net.au/pm, accessed
      8 March 2004.

28   www.web.macam98.ac.il, accessed 10 March 2004.

29   Fleay, op. cit., p. 277.

Chapter 2

1   www.rokebyprimary.tased.edu.au/NAIDOC Aboriginal students
      at Rokeby Primary School in southern Tasmania, with their
      teacher Grant Williams, created this story in the tradition of
      Dreamtime legends as a way of discovering more about their
      Aboriginal history through stories. The story formed part of the
      School's participation in NAIDOC (National Aboriginal Islander
      Day Observance Committee) Week 2003, a yearly celebration
      providing an opportunity for Australia's Indigenous people to
      display their culture and heritage to the rest of the Australian
      community.

2   Long, John, Archer, Michael, Flannery, Timothy, and Hand,
      Suzanne, *Prehistoric Mammals of Australia and New Guinea: One
      Hundred Million Years of Evolution*, Baltimore, Johns Hopkins
      University Press, 2002, p. 32.

3   ibid., p. 55.

4   Australian Museum Online, accessed 4 January 2004. www.am
      online.net.au/webinabox/fossils

5   Long et al., op. cit., p. 55.

6   www.environment.sa.gov.au/parks/naracoorte, accessed 5 January
      2004.

7   Wroe, Stephen, 'The Myth of Reptilian Domination', *Nature
      Australia*, Summer 2003–2004, p. 59.

8   Morrison, Reg, and Morrison, Maggie, *The Voyage of the Great
      Southern Ark*, Sydney, Lansdowne Press, 1988, p. 292.

9   Tasmanian evidence is instructive here. La Trobe University
      academic Dr Richard Cosgrove, a specialist in late Pleistocene archae-
      ology, examined over 48 000 bones from middens and cultural sites

202 | TASMANIAN DEVIL

across southwest Tasmania. They were overwhelmingly made up of Bennett's wallaby and wombat, the major Aboriginal food items for over 20 000 years. Just fourteen devil bones were found. That rules out any notion of overkill and instead emphasises good harvesting management. Cosgrove's work also found no evidence of human predation on megafauna, suggesting that they were extinct before human arrival at the southeast tip of the Australian continent and therefore succumbed to something other than overkill.

10 Based on analysis of a limestone hammer by Charles Dortch, Curator of Archaeology at the Western Australian Museum, using enhanced radiocarbon dating and optically stimulated luminescence methods.

11 Gill, Edmund D., 'The Australian Aborigines and the Tasmanian Devil', *Mankind*, 8 (1971), p. 59.

12 Noetling, Fritz, 'The Food of the Tasmanian Aborigines', *Papers & Proceedings of the Royal Society of Tasmania*, 1910, p. 281.

13 Flood, Josephine, *Archaeology of the Dreamtime*, Sydney, Collins, 1983, p. 62.

Chapter 3

1 Jones, Menna, 'Convergence in Ecomorphology and Guild Structure among Marsupial and Placental Carnivores', in Jones, Menna, Dickman, Chris and Archer, Mike (eds), *Predators with Pouches: The Biology of Carnivorous Marsupials*, Collingwood, Vic, CSIRO, 2003, p. 290. She cautions, however, that the success rate of such attacks is unknown.

2 ibid.

3 ibid.

4 Ewer, R. F., *The Carnivores*, London, Weidenfeld & Nicolson, 1973, p. 76.

5 Lord, Clive, 'Existing Tasmanian Marsupials', op. cit., 1927, p. 22.

6 www.wolverinefoundation.org, accessed 30 January 2005.

7   ibid.

8   ibid.

9   ibid.

10 www.napak.com/honey_badger, accessed 31 January 2005.

11 www.awf.org/wildlives/183, accessed 30 January 2005.

12 ibid.

13 ibid.

14 ibid.

15 Eisenberg, J.F., *The Mammalian Radiations*, Chicago, Ill., University of Chicago Press, 1981.

16 Menna Jones interview with David Owen, 1 October 2004.

17 ibid.

18 Strahan, Ronald (ed.), *The Mammals of Australia*, rev. edn, Chatswood, Reed Books, 1995, p. 60.

Chapter 4

1   www.abc.net.au/science/scribblygum, accessed 30 December 2003.

2   Fleay, David, 'The Tasmanian or Marsupial Devil—Its Habits and Family Life', op. cit., pp. 279–80.

3   Gilbert, Bill, *In God's Countries*, Omaha, University of Nebraska Press, 1984, p. 8. Gilbert earned considerable respect as a popular conservation and natural history writer and he travelled to Tasmania specifically to write the eighteen-page chapter on devils which appears in this book. He spoke to a number of people who could readily claim to know much about the devil.

4   Pemberton, David, 'Social Organisation and Behaviour of the Tasmanian Devil, *Sarcophilus harrisii*', thesis submitted in fulfilment of the requirements for the degree of Doctor of Philosophy in the Science Faculty, Zoology Department, Hobart, University of Tasmania, July 1990, p. 123. A total of 3788 traps were set in ten sessions for individual devil identification, trapping 328 males and 353 females, 554 and 515 times respectively. Most

devils became trap-shy but a few were caught many times. In respect of feeding, wallaby and wombat carcasses 'were placed in a paddock approximately fifteen metres from the edge of the tea-tree scrub running along a creek in the south of the study area. A hide was positioned fifteen metres from the carcass. The carcasses were always c. twenty kilograms in weight and were tied with thin wire to a stake embedded in the ground to prevent animals dragging them away. Lights were set up on the left and right hand side of the carcass to reduce the amount of light shining directly at the observer or the animals which usually approached the carcass from the bush edge . . . No animals left the carcass site when lights were switched on, and soon after intense interactions began there were animals moving within the white light, around the hide, and through the hide under the observer's chair' (p. 111).

5   ibid., p. 117. The 'yip' was identified subsequent to the completion of the thesis. Thylacines also had a 'yip' call.

6   ibid., p. 164.

Chapter 5

1   Harris, George Prideaux, 'Description of two new Species of Didelphis from Van Diemen's Land. By G. P. Harris, Esq. Communicated by the Right Honourable Sir Joseph Banks, Bart. K. B. Pres. R. S., H. M. L. S. Read April 21, 1807', in Linnean Society of London, *Transactions*, vol 9, 1808. X1, reproduced in *Letters of GP Harris 1803–1812*, edited by Barbara Hamilton-Arnold, London, Arden Press, 1994, p. 90.

2   Gould, John, *Mammals of Australia*, 1863, quoted in Joan M. Dixon (ed.), *The Best of Gould's Mammals*, Sydney, Macmillan, (rev. edn) 1984, p. 44.

3   Meredith, Louisa Anne, *Tasmanian Friends and Foes: Feathered, Furred and Finned; A Family Chronicle of Country Life, Natural History, and Veritable Adventure*, Hobart, J. Walch & Sons, 1880, pp. 63–5.

4 The island's Indigenous people were subject to near-genocide. Within 30 years of white settlement the nine tribes had been decimated through armed conflict, introduced diseases and dispersion. Billy was William Lanne, the last full-blood Aboriginal male, whose body was mutilated after death as part of a grisly conflict for possession between Tasmania's Royal Society and the Royal College of Surgeons in England. Truganini became celebrated as the last full-blood Tasmanian Aborigine. She died in 1876 and her skeleton was displayed in the Tasmanian Museum for many years, then kept hidden there. The Museum returned it to the Aboriginal community in 1976 and she was finally laid to rest in a ceremony on the waters of the D'Entrecasteaux Channel. Enlightened though she was in her time, Mary Roberts' casual use of these names is a sure indicator that notions of romantic savages still beat strongly in the Empire's bosom.

5 Roberts, Mary G., 'The Keeping and Breeding of Tasmanian Devils (*Sarcophilus harrisii*)', *Proceedings of the Zoological Society of London*, 1915, pp. 1–7.

6 ibid.

7 ibid.

8 Flynn, T. T., 'Contributions to a Knowledge of the Anatomy and Development of the Marsupiala [:] No. I. The Genitalia of *Sarcophilus satanicus*', *Proceedings of the Linnean Society of New South Wales,* vol. xxxv, Part 4, 30 November 1910. [Issued 1 March 1911], p. 873.

9 ibid.

10 ibid., p. 874.

11 Guiler, Eric, 'The Beaumaris Zoo in Hobart', *Tasmanian Historical Research Association Papers and Proceedings*, vol. 33, no. 4, December 1986, p. 128.

12 Lord, Clive, 'Existing Tasmanian Marsupials', *Royal Society of Tasmania Papers & Proceedings*, Hobart, 1927, p. 22.

13 ibid., p. 24.

Chapter 6

1 Brogden, Stanley, *Tasmanian Journey*, Melbourne, Morris & Walker for Pioneer Tours, 1948, p. 79.

2 Guiler, Eric, *The Enthusiastic Amateurs: The Animals and Birds Protection Board 1929–1971*, Sandy Bay, E. R. Guiler, 1999, p. 73.

3 The published results are in Guiler, E. R., 'Observations on the Tasmanian Devil, *Sarcophilus harrisii* (Dasyuridae: Marsupiala) at Granville Harbour, 1966–75', *Papers and Proceedings of the Royal Society of Tasmania*, vol. 112, 1978, Hobart, The Society, 1978, pp. 161–88. See also Guiler, E. R. and Heddle, R. W. L., 'Observations on the Tasmanian Devil, *Sarcophilus harrisii* (Dasyuridae: Marsupiala). 1. Numbers, home range, movements and food in two populations', *Australian Journal of Zoology*, 18(1), 1970, pp. 49–62.

4 *Australian Wild Life: Journal of the Wild Life Preservation Society*, vol. 3, no. 3, March 1958, Sydney, The Society, 1958, p. 14.

5 ibid.

6 *Australian Wild Life*, op. cit., vol. 4, no. 2, 1962, pp. 30–2.

7 *Australian Outdoors*, November 1961, Sydney, The Society, p. 36.

8 ibid., p. 37.

9 Bauer, Jack, 'Protection That Doesn't Protect', *Australian Outdoors*, November 1961, Sydney, The Society, pp. 36–41.

Chapter 7

1 Guiler, E. R., 'Observations on the Tasmanian Devil', p. 169.

2 ibid., p. 177.

3 ibid., p. 183.

4 *The Mercury*, 9 August 1966, p. 6. The area covered a 'fifty-mile radius' from Tooms Lake in the east to Interlaken across the Western Tiers, and south to Swansea.

5 *The Mercury*, 15 January 1972, p. 4.

6 *The Mercury*, 1 July 1972, p. 3.

7 Guiler, Eric, 'Tasmanian Devils and Agriculture', *Tasmanian Journal of Agriculture*, May 1970, p. 137.

8   *Launceston Examiner*, 28 January 1987, p. 3.

9   *Tasmanian Country*, 26 June 1987, p. 2.

10 *The Mercury*, 6 August 1975, p. 14.

11 'Tasmania. Ministerial News Release No. 1521, October 27, 1984.'

12 *The Mercury*, 2 February 1988, p. 1.

13 *The Mercury*, 16 October 1985, p. 1. Pam Clarke went on to become a leading world campaigner against the practice of battery hen egg production, for which she has an impressively long record of arrests and court appearances. In the leadup to the Sydney 2000 Olympic Games she gained considerable publicity for her campaign by saying that its official logo looked like 'a sad chook'.

14 *The Mercury*, 17 October 1985, pp. 1–2. The B.Sc. (Hons) thesis in question: 'The Cranial Anatomy and Thermoregulatory Physiology of the Tasmanian Devil, *Sarcophilus harrisii* (Marsupiala: Dasyuridae)', 1984, by Syed K. H. Shah, University of Tasmania, Hobart.

15 *The Mercury*, 7 July 1988, p. 1.

16 *The Sunday Tasmanian*, 23 July 1988, p. 5.

17 Mooney, Nick, 'The Devil you know', *Leatherwood: Tasmania's Journal of Discovery*, vol. 1, no. 3, Winter 1992, Hobart, Allan Moult, 1992, pp. 54–61.

Chapter 8

1   Virgis, Toren, interview with David Owen, 6 September 2004.

2   ibid.

3   ibid.

4   ibid.

5   Anderson, Angela, interview with David Owen, 24 January 2004.

6   www.kidszoo.com, accessed 10 April 2004.

7   The interview was conducted between 7 and 9 April in 2004.

8   Email dated 19 May 2004.

Chapter 9

1   Flynn, Errol, *My Wicked, Wicked Ways*, Cutchogue, New York, Buccaneer Books, 1976. Typical of the larrikin style of the book, Errol also refers to his father as 'just a tall hunk of scholarship' (p. 19).

2   Flynn, T. T., 'Contributions to a Knowledge of the Anatomy and Development of the Marsupiala [:] No. I. The Genitalia of *Sarcophilus Satanicus*', *Proceedings of the Linnean Society of New South Wales,* vol. xxxv, Part 4, 30 November 1910. [Issued 1 March 1911], p. 873.

3   Norman, Don, *Errol Flynn: The Tasmanian Story*, Hobart, W. N. Hurst & E. L. Metcalf, 1981, p. 4.

4   Flynn, Errol, op. cit., p. 24.

5   ibid., p. 104.

6   Jack Warner, quoted in *Hollywood Be Thy Name: The Warner Brothers Story*, by Cass Warner Sperling, Rocklin, CA, Prima, 1994, p. 195.

7   Flynn, Errol, op. cit., p. 168.

8   Warner, op. cit., p. xi.

9   ibid., p. 7 and p. 343.

10 Jones' inspiration for the coyote—a scavenging carnivore—came from an earlier creative interpretation: 'I first became interested in the Coyote while devouring Mark Twain's *Roughing It* at the age of seven. I had heard of the coyote only in passing references from passing adults and thought of it—if I thought of it at all—as a sort of dissolute collie. As it turned out, that's just about what a coyote is, and no one saw it more clearly than Mark Twain[:] "The coyote is a long, slim, sick and sorry-looking skeleton, with a gray wolf-skin stretched over it, a tolerably bushy tail that forever sags down with a despairing expression of forsakenness and misery, a furtive and evil eye, and a long, sharp face, with slightly lifted lip and exposed teeth. He has a general slinking expression all over. The coyote is a living, breathing allegory of Want. He is *always*

hungry. He is always poor, out of luck and friendless . . . He does not mind going a hundred miles to breakfast, and a hundred and fifty to dinner, because he is sure to have three or four days between meals . . ."' Jones, Chuck, *Chuck Amuck: the Life and Times of an Animated Cartoonist*, New York, Farrar, Straus & Giroux, 1989, pp. 34–5. (Twain visited the Tasmanian Museum and Art Gallery in 1897. He seemed to have difficulty identifying a Tasmanian devil and oddly referred to a highly predatory Tasmanian sheep-killing parrot that feasted only on its victims' kidney fat. He presumably meant the Kea, a scavenging carniverous parrot found only in New Zealand.)

11 Sandler, Kevin S. (ed.), *Reading the Rabbit: Explorations in Warner Bros. Animation*, New Brunswick, NJ, Rutgers University Press, 1998, p. 7.

12 Jones, op. cit., p. 109.

13 Beck, Jerry and Friedwald, Will, *Warner Bros. Animation Art: the Characters, the Creators, the Limited Editions*, Westport, CT, Hugh Lauter Levin Associates Inc/WB Worldwide Publishing, 1997, pp. 74–5.

14 ibid., pp. 129–30.

15 www.errolflynn.net/Filmography, accessed 30 December 2003.

16 Bevilacqua, Simon, *Sunday Tasmanian*, 10 May 1998, p. 7.

17 Taz looks not unlike a very young devil, which has a disproportionately big head and tucked-in, obscure limbs.

18 Lenburg, Jeff, *The Encyclopedia of Animated Cartoons*, 2nd edn, New York, Facts on File, 1999, p. 142.

19 Grant, John, *Masters of Animation*, London, BT Batsford, p. 154.

20 Jones, op. cit., pp. 92, 93.

Chapter 10

1 McCorry, Kevin, http://looney.toonzone.net/articles/tazarticle.html, accessed 14 June 2004.

2 Sandler, Kevin S. (ed.), *Reading the Rabbit: Explorations in Warner*

Bros. Animation, New Brunswick NJ, Rutgers University Press, 1998, p. 177.

3   Bevilacqua, Simon, *Sunday Tasmanian*, 28 September 1997.

4   ibid., p. 6.

5   ibid., p. 7.

6   ibid., pp. 1, 6.

7   ibid., p. 6.

8   ibid., p. 6.

9   *Sunday Tasmanian*, 5 October 1997, p. 3.

10   ibid., pp. 14, 15, 45.

11   *Hansard*, 15 October 1997. Hobart, Parliament of Tasmania, October 1997.

12   *Sunday Tasmanian*, 10 May 1998, p. 3.

13   *Hansard*, 15 October 1997.

Chapter 11

1   Meredith, Louisa Anne, *My Home in Tasmania, During a Residency of Nine Years*, London, John Murray, 1852, p. 106.

2   Gould, John, *Mammals of Australia*, 1863, quoted in Joan M. Dixon (ed.), *The Best of Gould's Mammals*, Sydney, Macmillan, (rev. edn) 1984, p. 44.

3   *The Mercury*, November 1910, p. 64.

4   Guiler, Eric R., 'The Former Distribution and Decline of the Thylacine', in *The Australian Journal of Science*, vol. 23, no. 7, 21 January 1961, p. 209.

5   Lord, Clive, 'Notes on the Mammals of Tasmania', op. cit., p. 45.

6   Lord, Clive, 'Existing Tasmanian Marsupials', op. cit., p. 22.

7   Lord, Clive E. and Scott, Herbert Hedley, *A Synopsis of the Vertebrate Animals of Tasmania*, [London], Oldham, Hobart, Beddome & Meredith, 1924, p. 267.

8   Flynn, T. T., 'Report of Ralston Professor of Biology for the Year ending June 30th 1919', p. 4. University of Tasmania, Morris Miller Library Special and Rare Collections.

9 Willoughby, Howard, *Australian Pictures Drawn With Pen and Pencil*, London, The Religious Tract Society, 1886, p. 182.

10 Brown, Bob, 'Interview with Mr Lewis Stevenson, 69 Guy Street, Launceston', 1 December 1972, Collection Queen Victoria Museum and Art Gallery.

11 *The Mercury*, 3 November 1910, p. 64.

12 Kelly, Androo, *The Mercury*, 1 September 2003, p. 11.

13 A more scientific definition of a retrovirus: 'Viral insertion into host cell DNA can cause considerable disruption to the genome, and viral promoters can drive the transcription of cellular genes that may otherwise be inactive. A consequence of this lifecycle is the ability to trigger neoplasia [tumours] through insertional mutation or proto-oncogene [cancer-causing] activation. Some retroviruses, through faulty transcription, have also captured cellular oncogenes within their genomes and these oncogenes, when inserted into a new cell, may cause neoplastic transformation. Viral proteins of some retroviruses are also known to have immunosuppressive properties, although the precise mechanisms of immunosuppression are less well understood.' Hanger, Jon, McKee, Jeff, Tarlington, Rachael and Yates, Amanda, 'Cancer and Haematological Disease in Koalas: a Clinical and Virological Update', p. 8. Paper presented at the Devil Facial Tumour Disease Workshop, Sir Raymond Ferrall Centre, University of Tasmania, Newnham, 14 October 2003.

14 *The Mercury*, 2 September 2003, p. 5.

15 'Research into the Tasmanian Devil Facial Tumour Disease (DFTD)[:] Progress Report', Tasmania, Department of Primary Industries, Water and Environment (DPIWE), January 2005, p. 5.

16 *The Mercury*, 2 September 2003, p. 16.

17 *The Mercury*, 9 September 2003, p. 14.

18 *Sunday Tasmanian*, 3 October 2004, pp. 1, 8.

19 'Research into the Tasmanian Devil Facial Tumour Disease (DFTD)[:] Progress Report', op. cit., p. 27.

20 Loh, Dr Richmond, 'Tasmanian Devil (*Sarcophilus harrisii*) Facial Tumour (DFT)', paper prepared for the 14 October 2003 workshop, p. 2.

21 DPIWE general manager Alex Schaap, quoted in *The Mercury*, 29 October 2003, p. 2.

22 *Hansard*, Parliament of Tasmania, 29 October 2003.

23 Tweety, the cute little baby-talking yellow canary, and Sylvester, the ugly big lisping black-and-white cat, first came together in 1947. Director Friz Freling 'knew he had just united the Warner studio's own dream team. From that point on, it was Bird vs. Cat in an almost uncountable number of episodes, a struggle that carried them across six decades and the farthest corners of the globe. And it was always Sylvester's own deviousness and bad luck that did in him, while Tweety's childlike innocence (and brutal sense of self-preservation) kept him out of the cat's stomach.' Beck, Jerry and Friedwald, Will, *Warner Bros. Animation Art: the Characters, the Creators, the Limited Editions*, Westport, CT, Hugh Lauter Levin Associates Inc/WB Worldwide Publishing, 1997, pp. 115–6.

24 *The Mercury*, 13 April 2004, pp. 1–2.

25 The specialists: Menna Jones (evolutionary ecology and conservation of marsupial carnivores); Heather Hesterman (wildlife and captive breeding programs); Clare Hawkins (carnivorous mammals, Madagascan fossa ecology); Jason Wiersma (predatory birds, critical habitat surveys, Fox Taskforce, developer of the infra-red camera); Billie Lazenby (habitat assessments, small mammal ecology, Fox Taskforce, compiler of hair atlas of Tasmanian wildlife); Stephen Pyecroft (veterinary pathologist, Mount Pleasant group leader); Richmond Loh (veterinary pathologist, Murdoch University); Robyn Sharpe (veterinary pathologist); Nolan Fox (DNA repair mechanism related to human tumours); Ann Maree Pearce (genetics, dasyurids and cytogenetics).

26 Pemberton, David, 'Devil Facial Tumour: Tasmanian Devil

Survey, Table Mountain, Bothwell, January 2004', p. 4. [unpublished field notes]

27 Scammell, Dr Marcus, 'Environmental Problems [in] Georges Bay, Tasmania. Collated by Dr Marcus Scammell from information gathered, in particular, between February 2004 to June 2004', http://www.tfic.com.au/scammell_report_07.04.htm, accessed 11 September 2004.

28 Jim Bacon, quoted in *The Mercury*, 3 September 2003, p. 3.

SELECT BIBLIOGRAPHY

Beck, Jerry, and Friedwald, Will, *Warner Bros. Animation Art: the Characters, the Creators, the Limited Editions*, Westport, CT, Hugh Lauter Levin Associates Inc/WB Worldwide Publishing, 1997.

Brogden, Stanley, *Tasmanian Journey*, Melbourne, Morris & Walker for Pioneer Tours, 1948.

Eisenberg, John, *The Mammalian Radiations*, Chicago, University of Chicago Press, 1986.

Ewer, R. F., *The Carnivores*, London, Weidenfeld and Nicolson, 1973.

Farrand, John Jr., ed., *The Audubon Society Encyclopedia of Animal Life*, New York, Chanticleer Press, 1987 [Sixth Printing, 1988].

Flood, Josephine, *Archaeology of the Dreamtime*, Sydney, Collins, 1983.

Flynn, Errol, *My Wicked, Wicked Ways,* Cutchogue, New York, Buccaneer Books, 1976.

Gilbert, Bill, *In God's Countries*, Omaha, University of Nebraska Press, 1984.

Gould, John, *The Best of Gould's Mammals: Selections from* Mammals of Australia Volumes l, ll and lll, selected and introduced with modern commentaries by Joan Dixon, South Melbourne, Macmillan, 1977 (rev. edn 1984).

Grant, John, *Masters of Animation*, London, B. T. Batsford, 2001.

Green, R. H., *The Mammals of Tasmania*, Launceston, Foot & Playsted, 1973.

Grzimek, Bernhard, *Australians{:} Adventures with Animals and Men in Australia*, Translated by J. Maxwell Brownjohn, London-Sydney, Collins, 1967.

Guiler, Eric, *The Enthusiastic Amateurs: The Animals and Birds Protection Board 1929-1971*, Sandy Bay, E. R. Guiler, 1999.

Guiler, Eric, *Marsupials of Tasmania*, Hobart, Tasmanian Museum and Art Gallery, 1960.

Guiler, Eric, *The Tasmanian Devil*, Hobart, St David's Park Publishing, 1992.

Jones, Chuck, *Chuck Amuck: the Life and Times of an Animated Cartoonist*, New York, Farrar Straus Giroux, 1989.

Jones, Menna, Dickman, Chris, Archer, Mike, eds, *Predators with Pouches: the Biology of Carniverous Marsupials*, Collingwood, Vic., CSIRO, 2003.

Le Soeuf, W. H. Dudley, *Wildlife in Australia*, Christchurch [NZ], Melbourne, Whitcombe and Tombs, 1907.

Lenburg, Jeff, *The Encyclopedia of Animated Cartoons*, 2nd ed., New York, Facts on File, 1999.

Long, John, Archer, Michael, Flannery, Timothy, Hand, Suzanne, *Prehistoric Mammals of Australia and New Guinea: One Hundred Million Years of Evolution*, Baltimore, Johns Hopkins University Press, 2002.

Lord, Clive E., and Scott, Herbert Hedley, *A Synopsis of the Vertebrate Animals of Tasmania,* London, Oldham, Hobart, Beddome and Meredith, 1924.

Meredith, Louisa Anne, *My Home in Tasmania, During a Residency of Nine Years*, London, John Murray, 1852.

Meredith, Louisa Anne, *Tasmanian Friends and Foes: Feathered, Furred and Finned; A Family Chronicle of Country Life, Natural History, and Veritable Adventure*, Hobart, J Walch & Sons, 1880.

Mooney, Nick, 'The Devil you know', in *Leatherwood: Tasmania's Journal of Discovery*, Volume 1 Number 3, Winter 1992, Hobart, Allan Moult, 1992.

Morrison, Reg, and Morrison, Maggie, *The Voyage of the Great Southern Ark*, Sydney, Lansdowne Press, 1988.

Norman, Don, *Errol Flynn: The Tasmanian Story*, Hobart, W. N. Hurst and E. L. Metcalf, 1981.

Nowak, Ronald M., *Walker's Mammals of the World*, Baltimore, Johns Hopkins University Press, 1999.

Sandler, Kevin S., ed., *Reading the Rabbit: Explorations in Warner Bros. Animation,* New Brunswick, NJ, Rutgers University Press, 1998.

Sperling, Cass Warner, *Hollywood Be Thy Name: the Warner Brothers Story*, Rocklin, CA, Prima, 1994.

Strahan, Ronald, ed., *The Mammals of Australia*, rev. edn, Chatswood, Reed Books, 1995.

Taylor, James, comp., *Zoo: Studies From Nature*, Sydney, James Taylor, 1920.

Watts, Dave, *Tasmanian Mammals: A Field Guide*, Hobart, Tasmanian Conservation Trust, 1987.

Willoughby, Howard, *Australian Pictures Drawn With Pen and Pencil*, London, The Religious Tract Society, 1886.

Wroe, Stephen, 'The Myth of Reptilian Domination', in *Nature Australia*, Summer 2003-2004, p. 59.

www.wolverinefoundation.org

www.rokebyprimary.tased.edu.au/NAIDOC

www.napak.com/honey_badger

www.awf.org/wildlives

www.environment.sa.gov.au/parks/naracoorte

www.jonacohen.com/jersey_devil

www.errolflynn.net/Filmography

www.kidszoo.com

INDEX